MONSTER ORIGAMI

DUY

NGUYEN

New York / London
www.sterlingpublishing.com/kids

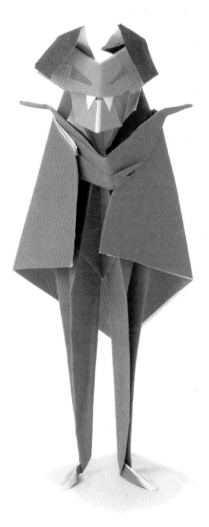

STERLING and the distinctive Sterling logo are registered trademarks of Sterling Publishing Co., Inc.

Library of Congress Cataloging-in-Publication Data

Nguyen, Duy, 1960-
  Monster origami / Duy Nguyen.
      p. cm.
  Includes index.
  ISBN-13: 978-1-4027-4014-5
  ISBN-10: 1-4027-4014-X
  1. Origami. I. Title.

TT870.N48635 2007
736'.982—dc22

                          2007003244

10 9 8 7 6 5 4 3 2 1

Published by Sterling Publishing Company, Inc
387 Park Avenue South, New York, NY 10016
© 2007 by Duy Nguyen
Distributed in Canada by Sterling Publishing
^c/o Canadian Manda Group, 165 Dufferin Street
Toronto, Ontario, Canada M6K 3H6
Distributed in the United Kingdom by GMC Distribution Services
Castle Place, 166 High Street, Lewes, East Sussex, England BN7 1XU
Distributed in Australia by Capricorn Link (Australia) Pty. Ltd.
P.O. Box 704, Windsor, NSW 2756, Australia

Printed in China

Sterling ISBN-13: 978-1-4027-4014-5
        ISBN-10: 1-4027-4014-X

For information about custom editions, special sales, premium and corporate purchases, please contact Sterling Special Sales Department at 800-805-5489 or specialsales@sterlingpub.com.

Contents

Preface

Years ago, when I first began to fold origami, I would look again and again at the instructions given in my borrowed book, trying to learn even the simplest folds. But I also looked ahead, studying the diagram showing the next step of whatever project I was folding, to see how it should look after the fold. As it turned out, looking ahead at the next step, the result of a fold, is a very good way for a beginner to learn origami. You will easily pick up this learning technique and many others as you follow the step-by-step directions given here for creating a menagerie of menacing monsters. So sit down, select some squares of paper, and discover the enjoyment of bringing creatures of horror from books and movies to new life in your hands.

Duy Nguyen

Basic Instructions

Paper: Paper used in traditional origami is thin, keeps a crease well, and folds flat. Packets of specially designed sheets, from 5 to 8 inches (13 to 21 cm) square, are available in various colors. You can also use plain white, solid-color, even wrapping paper with a design on only one side, and cut the paper to size. Be aware, though, that some papers stretch slightly in length or width, which can cause folding problems, while others tear easily.

Beginners or those concerned about working with smaller tight folds can also use larger paper sizes. While regular paper may be a bit heavy to allow the many tight folds used in creating small traditional origami figures, it is fine for practicing or working on larger projects.

Use same-size squares for working the multi-part figures in this book, unless other dimensions are provided.

Technique: Make each fold with care. Position the paper precisely, especially at the corners, and line the edges up before creasing. Once you are sure of the fold, use a fingernail to make a clean, flat crease.

For more complex folds, create "construction lines." Fold and unfold, using simple mountain and valley folds, to pre-crease. This creates guidelines, and the finished fold is more likely to match the one shown in the book. At this stage, folds that look different, because the angles aren't quite right, can throw you off. Don't get discouraged with your first efforts. In time, what your mind can create, your fingers can fashion.

Creativity: Once you are confident in your folding ability, try adjusting certain folds to shape each figure more to your liking. An arm reaching out, a threatening step forward, and your paper creature springs to chilling life.

Do add color and detail, too. Feel free to use markers, glue on bits and folds of paper, add props, and do whatever you like to make each figure special.

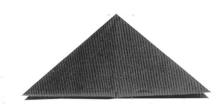

Symbols & Lines

Fold lines   valley   – – – – – – –   Fold then unfold   ←———→

                 mountain   –·–·–·–·–

Cut line   ++++++++++++++   Pleat fold
(repeated folding)

Turn over or rotate   Crease line   ————

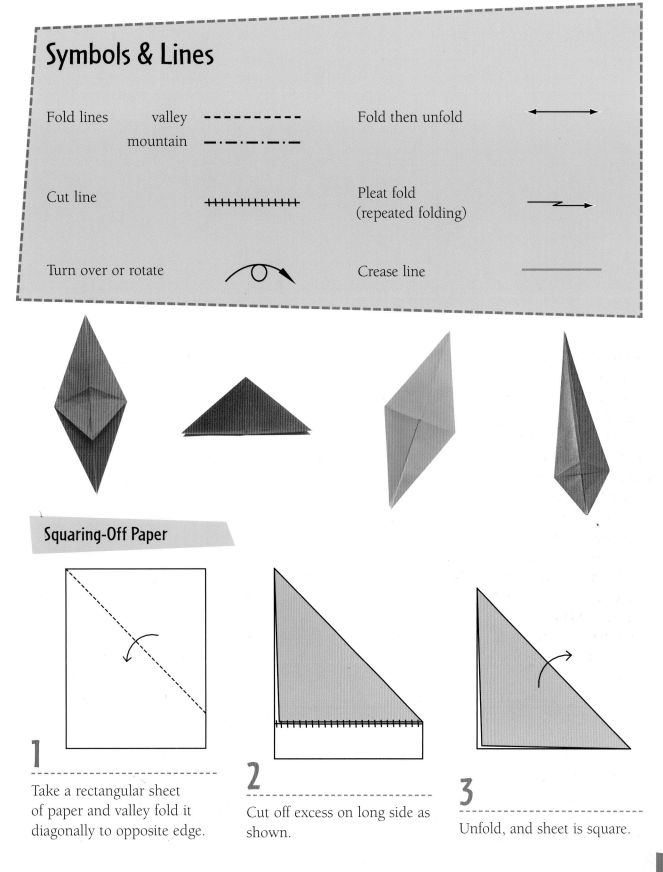

Squaring-Off Paper

1

Take a rectangular sheet of paper and valley fold it diagonally to opposite edge.

2

Cut off excess on long side as shown.

3

Unfold, and sheet is square.

Basic Folds

Kite Fold

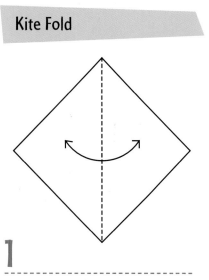

1

Fold and unfold a square diagonally, making a center crease.

2

Fold both sides in to the center crease.

3

This is a kite form.

Valley Fold - - - - - - - - - - - - - - - - -

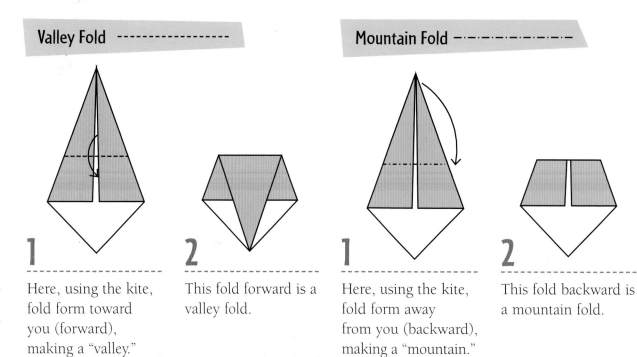

1

Here, using the kite, fold form toward you (forward), making a "valley."

2

This fold forward is a valley fold.

Mountain Fold - - · - - · - - · - - · -

1

Here, using the kite, fold form away from you (backward), making a "mountain."

2

This fold backward is a mountain fold.

6

Inside Reverse Fold

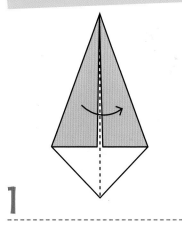

1
Starting here with a kite, valley fold kite closed.

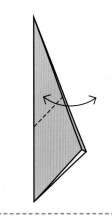

2
Valley fold as marked to crease, then unfold.

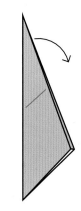

3
Pull tip in direction of arrow.

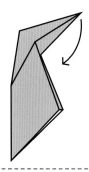

4
Appearance before completion.

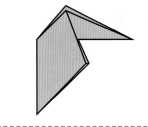

5
You've made an inside reverse fold.

Outside Reverse Fold

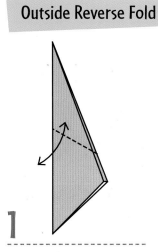

1
Using closed kite, valley fold, unfold.

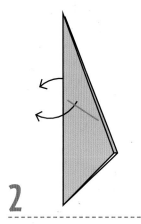

2
Fold inside out, as shown by arrows.

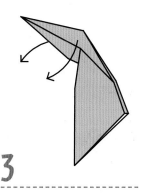

3
Appearance before completion.

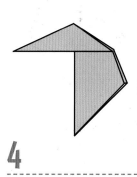

4
You've made an outside reverse fold.

Basic Folds

Pleat Fold

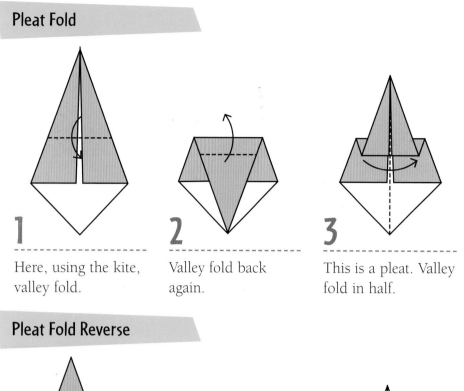
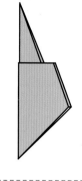

1
Here, using the kite, valley fold.

2
Valley fold back again.

3
This is a pleat. Valley fold in half.

4
You've made a pleat fold.

Pleat Fold Reverse

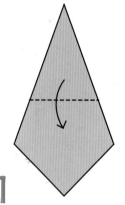
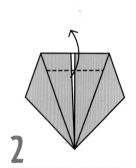
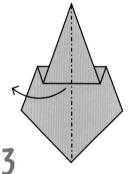
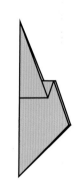

1
Here, using the kite form backwards, valley fold.

2
Valley fold back again for pleat.

3
Mountain fold form in half.

4
This is a pleat fold reverse.

Squash Fold I

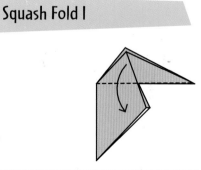
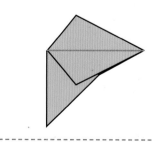

1
Using inside reverse, valley fold one side.

2
This is a squash fold I.

Squash Fold II

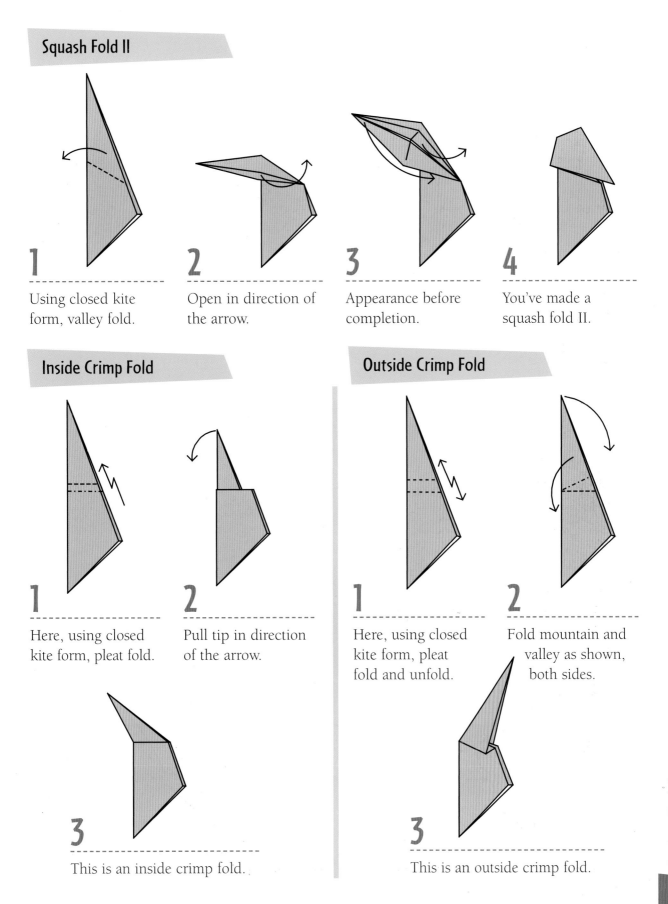

1 Using closed kite form, valley fold.

2 Open in direction of the arrow.

3 Appearance before completion.

4 You've made a squash fold II.

Inside Crimp Fold

1 Here, using closed kite form, pleat fold.

2 Pull tip in direction of the arrow.

3 This is an inside crimp fold.

Outside Crimp Fold

1 Here, using closed kite form, pleat fold and unfold.

2 Fold mountain and valley as shown, both sides.

3 This is an outside crimp fold.

Base Folds

Base folds are basic forms that do not in themselves produce origami, but serve as a basis, or jumping-off point, for a number of creative origami figures—some quite complex. As when beginning other crafts, learning to fold these base folds is not the most exciting part of origami. They are, however, easy to do, and will help you with your technique. They also quickly become rote, so much so that you can do many using different-colored papers while you are watching television or your mind is elsewhere. With completed base folds handy, if you want to quickly work up a form or are suddenly inspired with an idea for an original, unique figure, you can select an appropriate base fold and swiftly bring a new creation to life.

Base Fold I

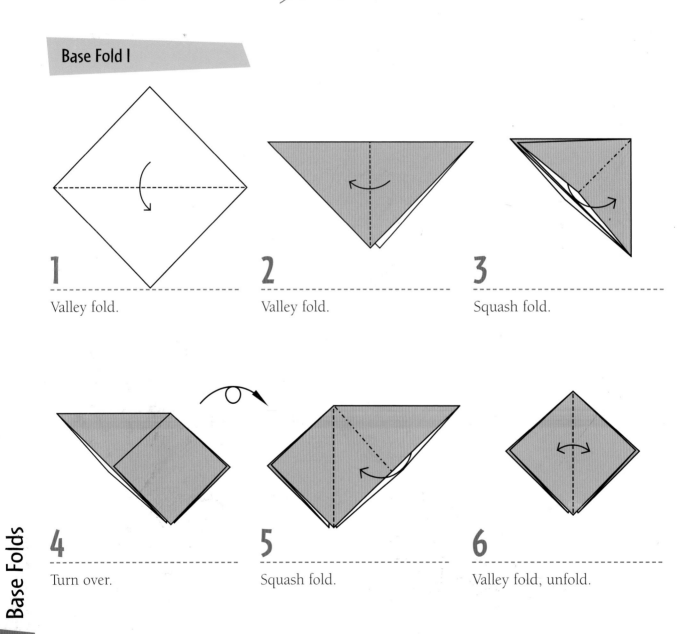

1 Valley fold.

2 Valley fold.

3 Squash fold.

4 Turn over.

5 Squash fold.

6 Valley fold, unfold.

7

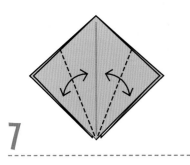

Valley folds, unfold.

8

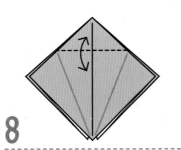

Valley fold, unfold.

9

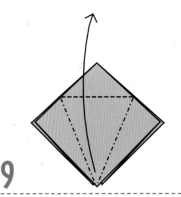

Pull in direction of arrow, folding inward at sides.

10

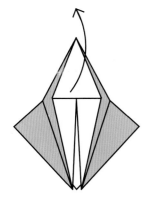

Appearance before completion of fold.

11

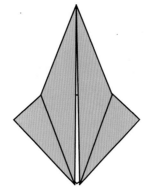

Completed Base Fold I.

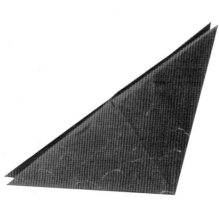

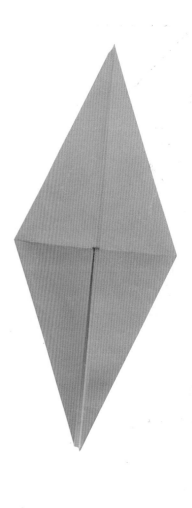

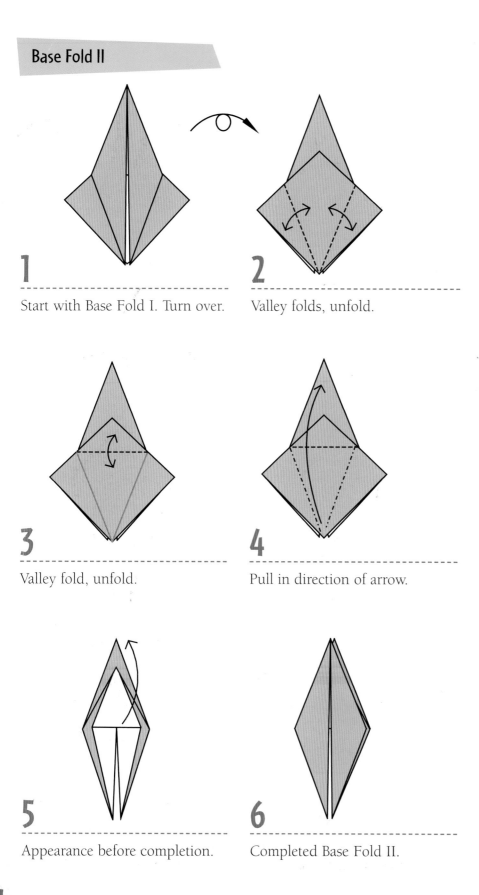

1
Start with Base Fold I. Turn over.

2
Valley folds, unfold.

3
Valley fold, unfold.

4
Pull in direction of arrow.

5
Appearance before completion.

6
Completed Base Fold II.

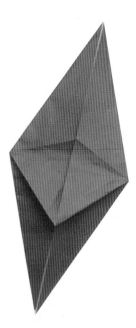

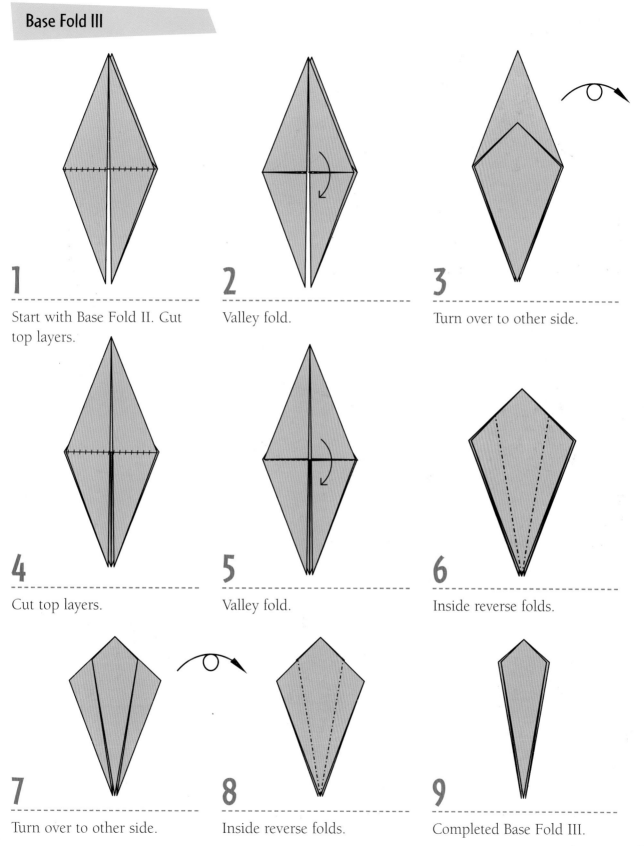

1

Start with Base Fold II. Cut top layers.

2

Valley fold.

3

Turn over to other side.

4

Cut top layers.

5

Valley fold.

6

Inside reverse folds.

7

Turn over to other side.

8

Inside reverse folds.

9

Completed Base Fold III.

1

Valley fold rectangle in half as shown. (Note: Size of Base Fold IV paper is variable based on needs of project.)

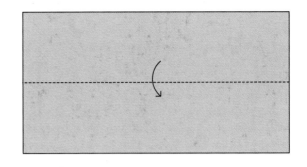

2

Valley fold in direction of arrow.

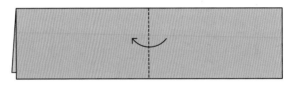

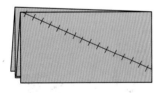

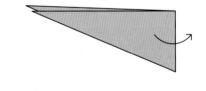

3

Make cut as shown.

4

Unfold.

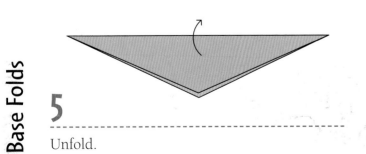

5

Unfold.

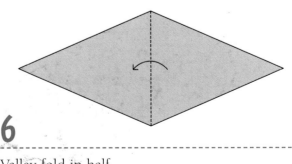

6

Valley fold in half.

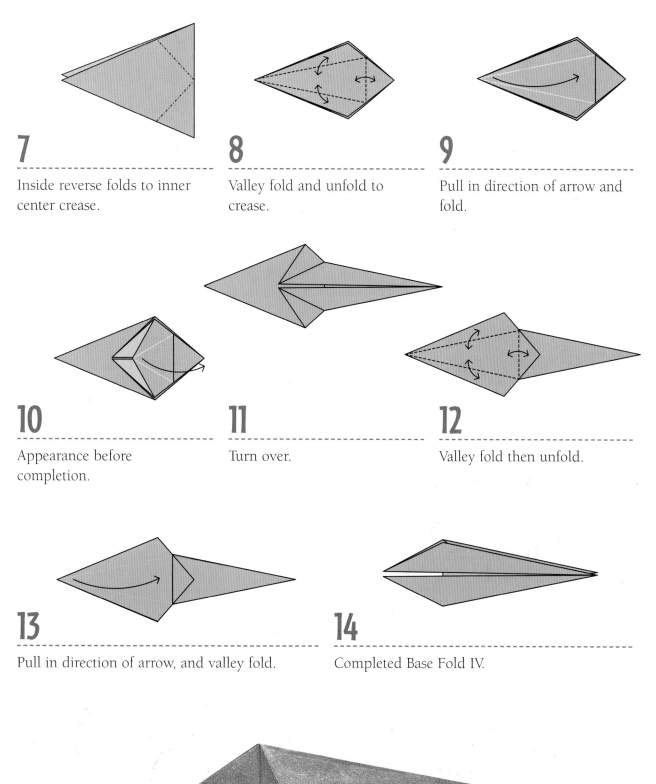

7

Inside reverse folds to inner center crease.

8

Valley fold and unfold to crease.

9

Pull in direction of arrow and fold.

10

Appearance before completion.

11

Turn over.

12

Valley fold then unfold.

13

Pull in direction of arrow, and valley fold.

14

Completed Base Fold IV.

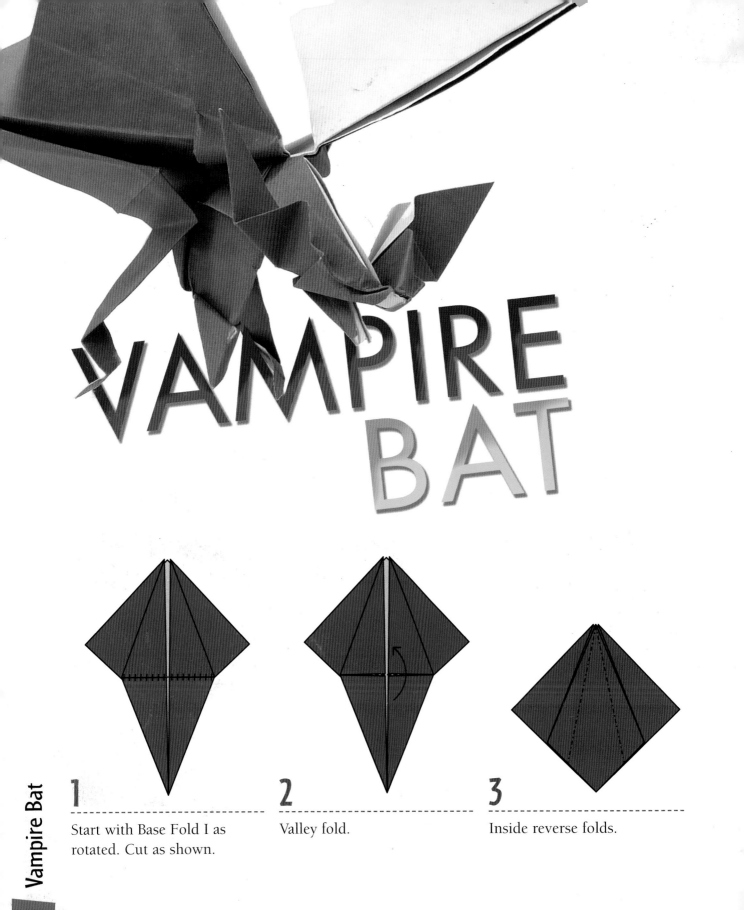

VAMPIRE BAT

1

Start with Base Fold I as rotated. Cut as shown.

2

Valley fold.

3

Inside reverse folds.

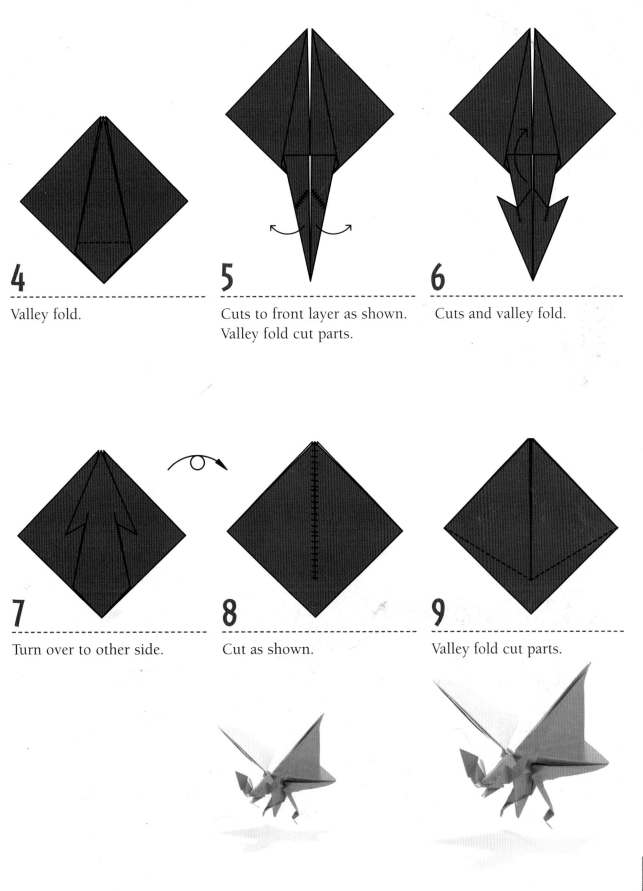

4

Valley fold.

5

Cuts to front layer as shown.
Valley fold cut parts.

6

Cuts and valley fold.

7

Turn over to other side.

8

Cut as shown.

9

Valley fold cut parts.

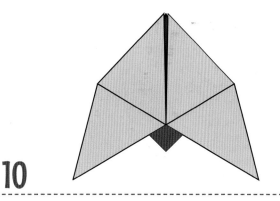

10

Turn over to other side.

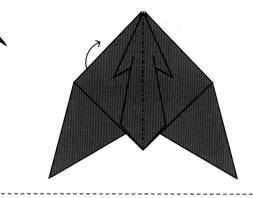

11

Mountain fold in half.

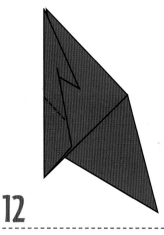

12

Outside reverse fold.

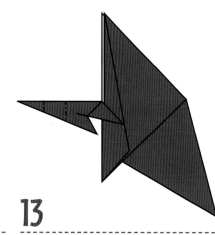

13

Crimp fold.

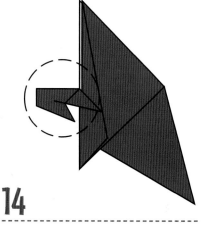

14

See close-ups for more detail.

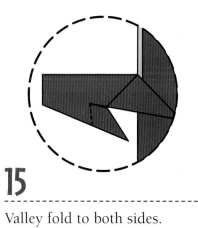

15

Valley fold to both sides.

16

Repeat.

17

Repeat.

18

Repeat.

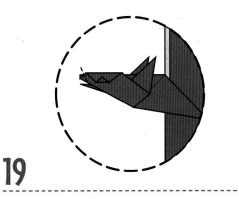

19

Outside reverse fold.

20

Pull and squash into position.

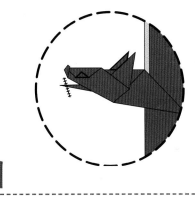

21

Cut as shown.

22

Valley fold both sides.

23

Back to full view.

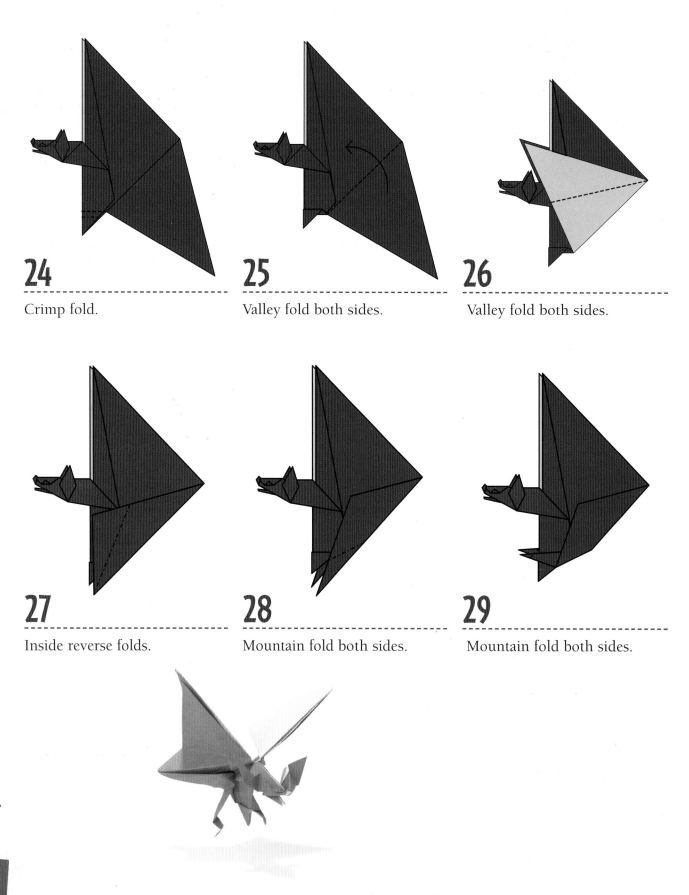

24
Crimp fold.

25
Valley fold both sides.

26
Valley fold both sides.

27
Inside reverse folds.

28
Mountain fold both sides.

29
Mountain fold both sides.

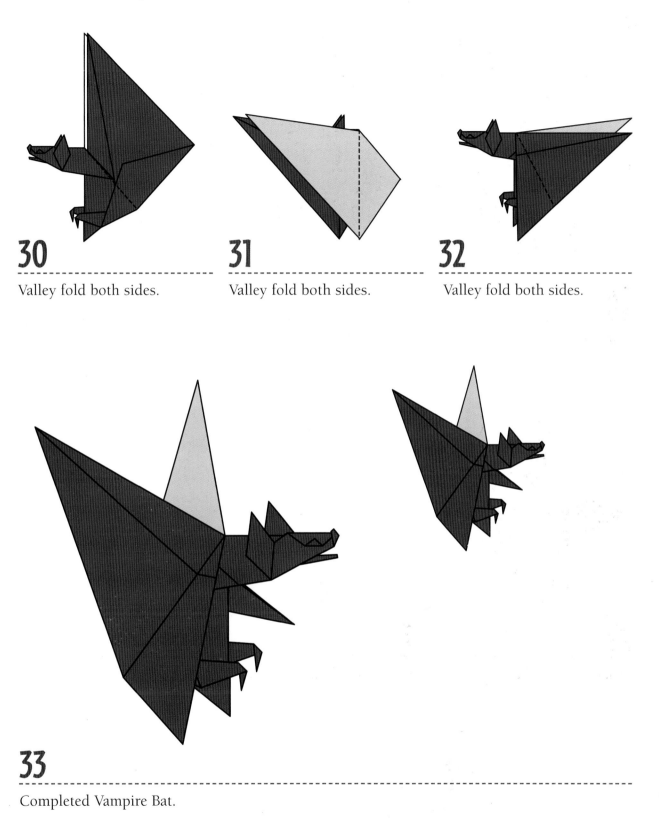

30

Valley fold both sides.

31

Valley fold both sides.

32

Valley fold both sides.

33

Completed Vampire Bat.

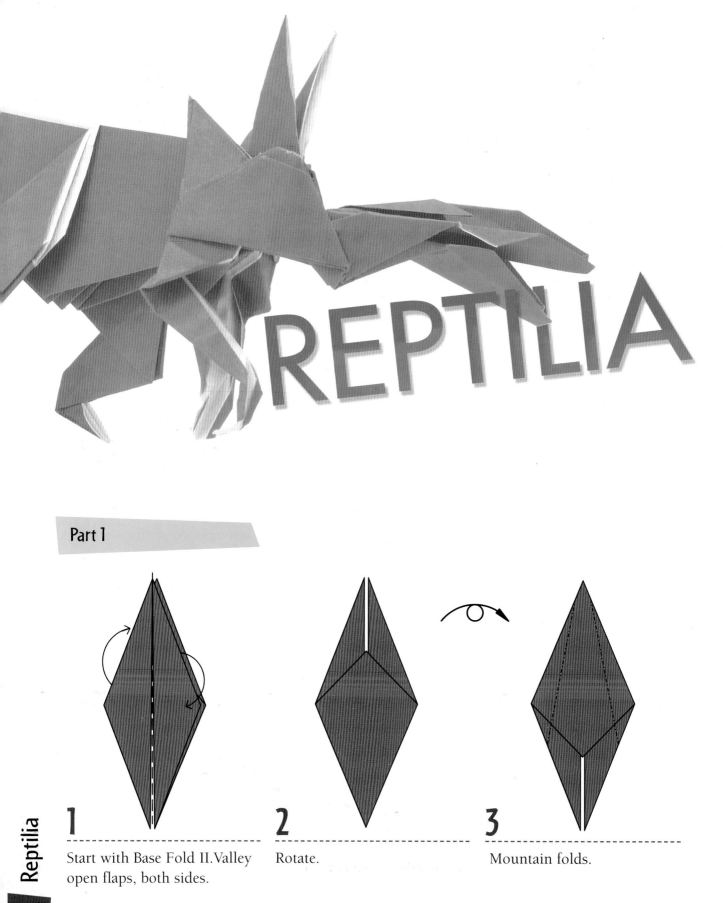

REPTILIA

Part 1

1

Start with Base Fold II. Valley open flaps, both sides.

2

Rotate.

3

Mountain folds.

22

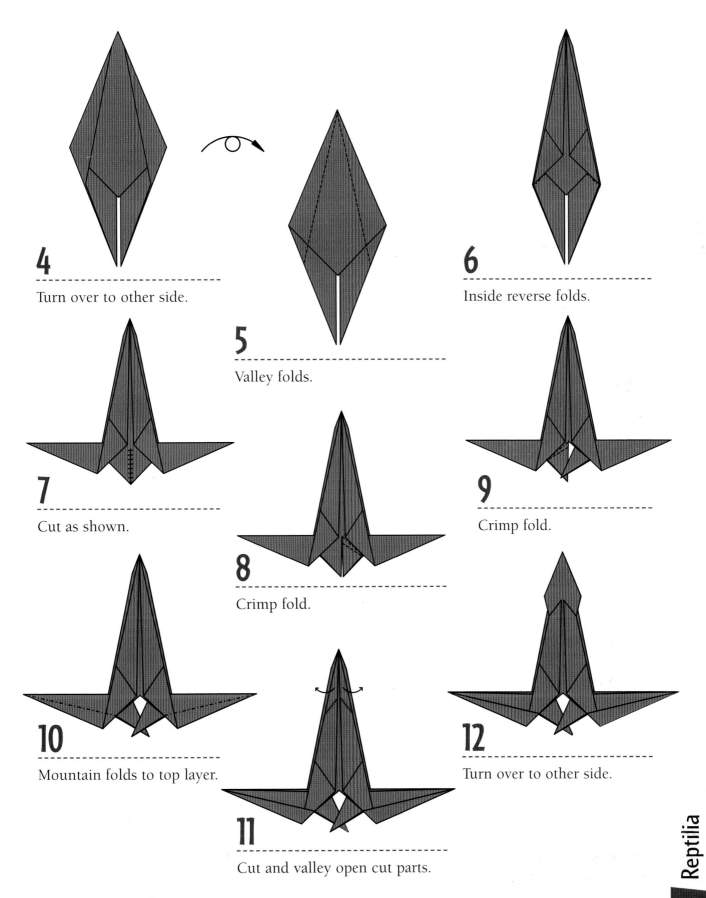

4

Turn over to other side.

5

Valley folds.

6

Inside reverse folds.

7

Cut as shown.

8

Crimp fold.

9

Crimp fold.

10

Mountain folds to top layer.

11

Cut and valley open cut parts.

12

Turn over to other side.

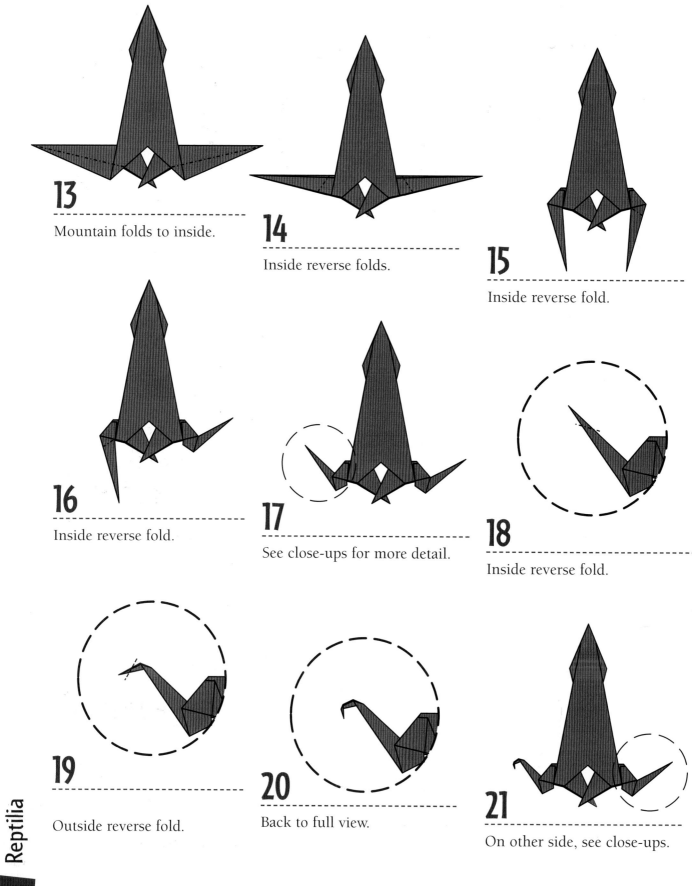

13 Mountain folds to inside.

14 Inside reverse folds.

15 Inside reverse fold.

16 Inside reverse fold.

17 See close-ups for more detail.

18 Inside reverse fold.

19 Outside reverse fold.

20 Back to full view.

21 On other side, see close-ups.

22

Inside reverse folds.

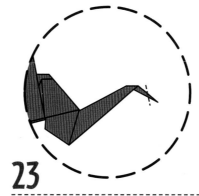

23

Outside reverse fold.

24

Back to full view.

25

Mountain fold.

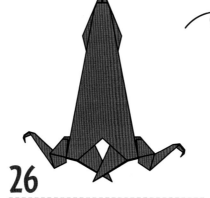

26

Turn over to other side.

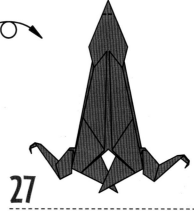

27

Valley fold.

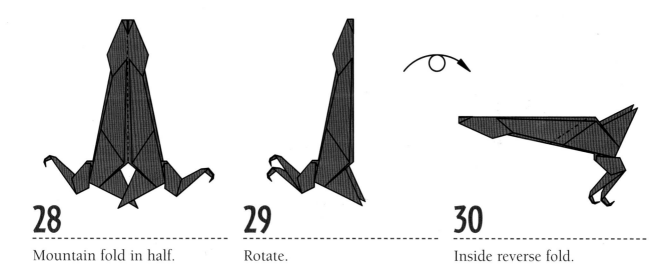

28

Mountain fold in half.

29

Rotate.

30

Inside reverse fold.

31

Inside reverse fold.

32

Inside reverse fold.

33

Valley fold to both sides.

34

Completed part 1 of Reptilia.

Part 2

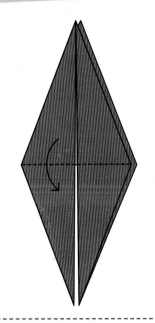

1

Start with Base Fold II. Valley fold.

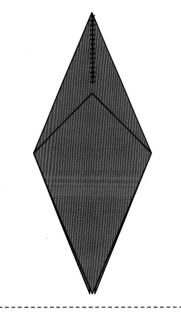

2

Cut as shown.

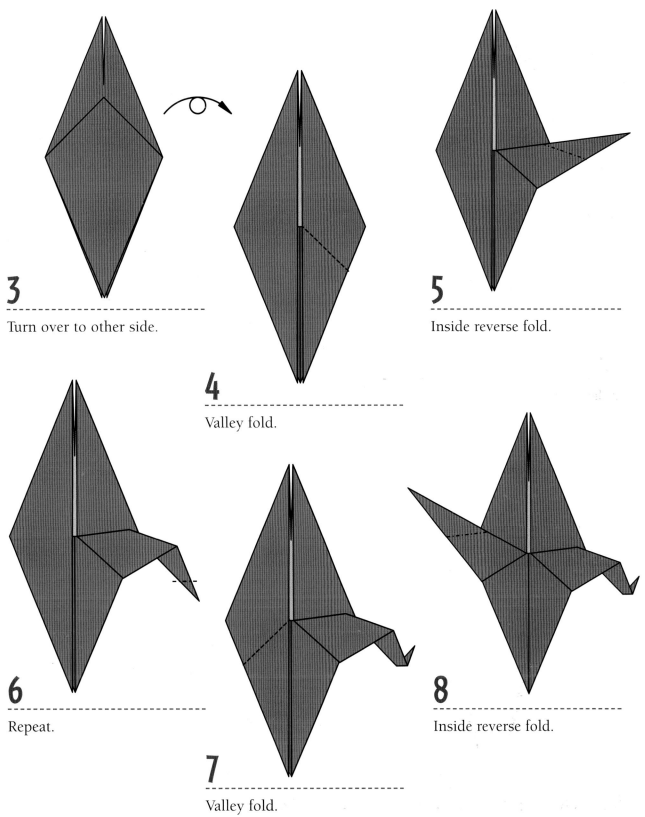

3
Turn over to other side.

4
Valley fold.

5
Inside reverse fold.

6
Repeat.

7
Valley fold.

8
Inside reverse fold.

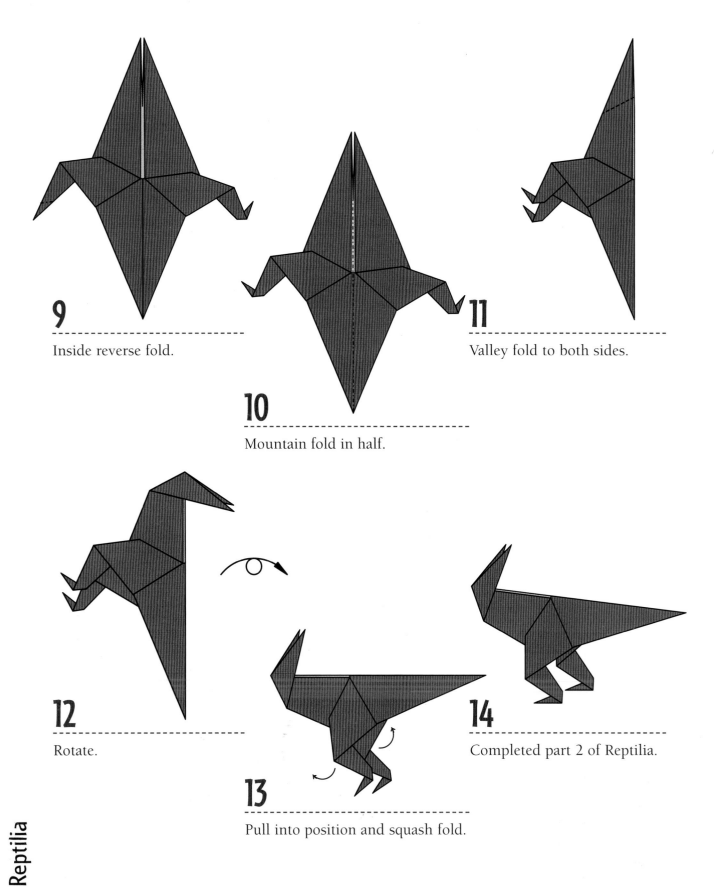

9

Inside reverse fold.

10

Mountain fold in half.

11

Valley fold to both sides.

12

Rotate.

13

Pull into position and squash fold.

14

Completed part 2 of Reptilia.

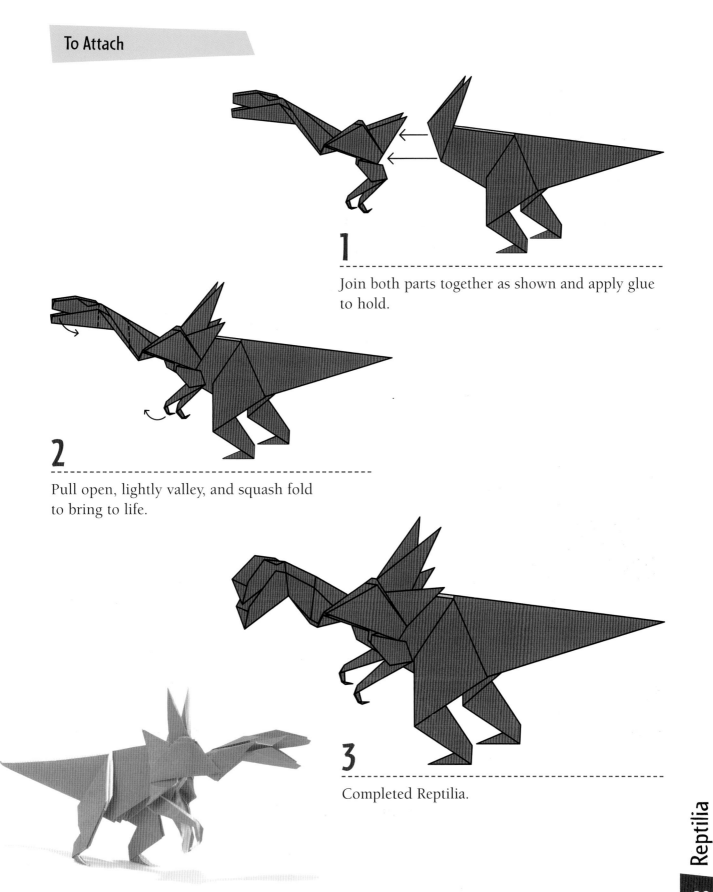

1

Join both parts together as shown and apply glue to hold.

2

Pull open, lightly valley, and squash fold to bring to life.

3

Completed Reptilia.

Reptilia

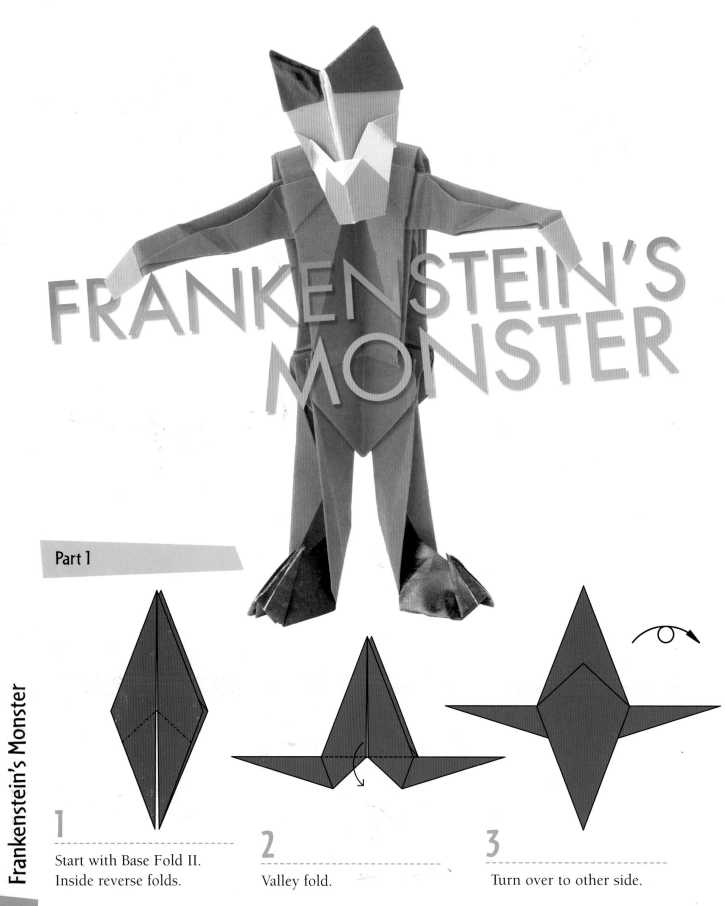

FRANKENSTEIN'S MONSTER

Part 1

1
Start with Base Fold II.
Inside reverse folds.

2
Valley fold.

3
Turn over to other side.

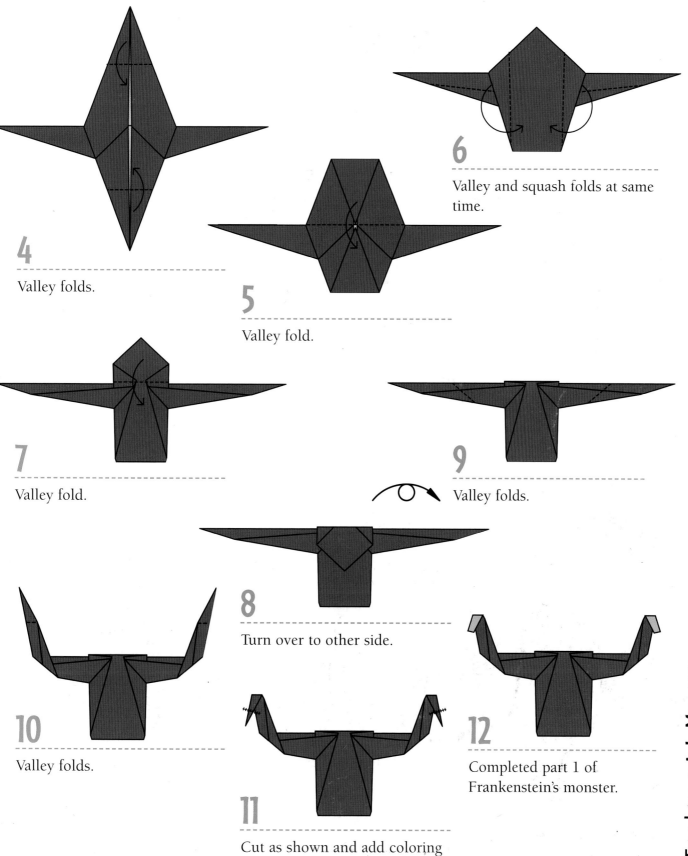

4

Valley folds.

5

Valley fold.

6

Valley and squash folds at same time.

7

Valley fold.

8

Turn over to other side.

9

Valley folds.

10

Valley folds.

11

Cut as shown and add coloring

12

Completed part 1 of Frankenstein's monster.

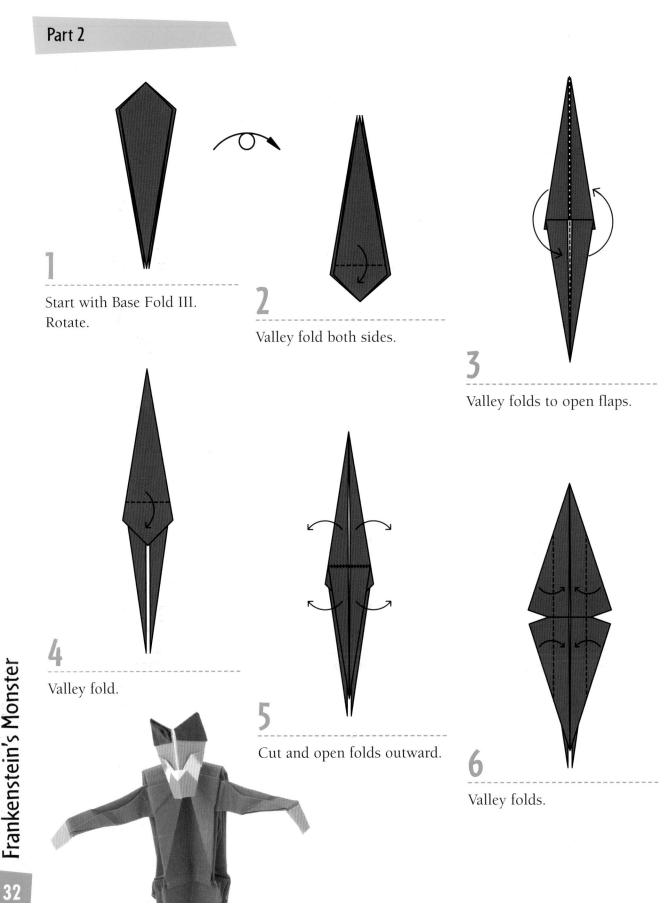

Part 2

1

Start with Base Fold III.
Rotate.

2

Valley fold both sides.

3

Valley folds to open flaps.

4

Valley fold.

5

Cut and open folds outward.

6

Valley folds.

Frankenstein's Monster

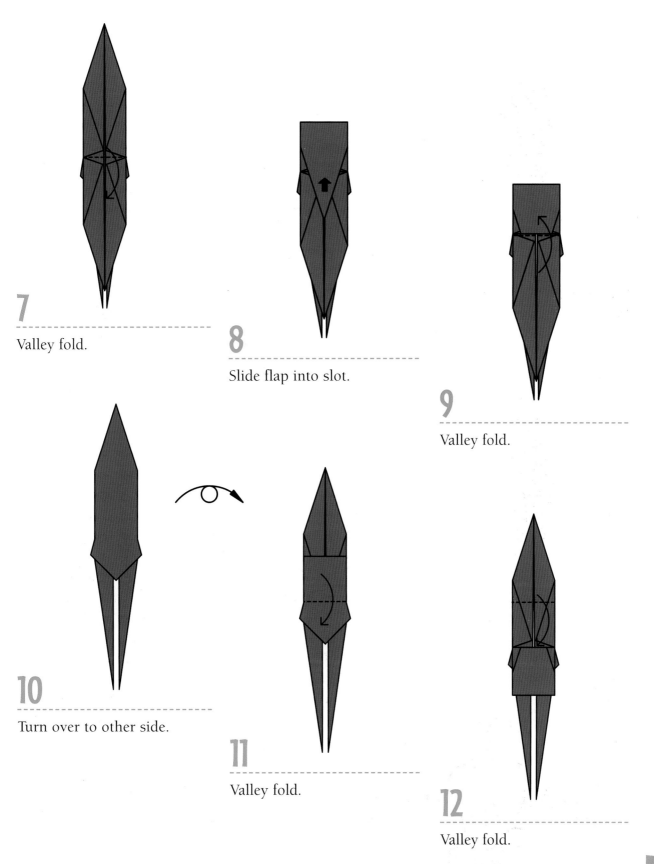

7

Valley fold.

8

Slide flap into slot.

9

Valley fold.

10

Turn over to other side.

11

Valley fold.

12

Valley fold.

Frankenstein's Monster

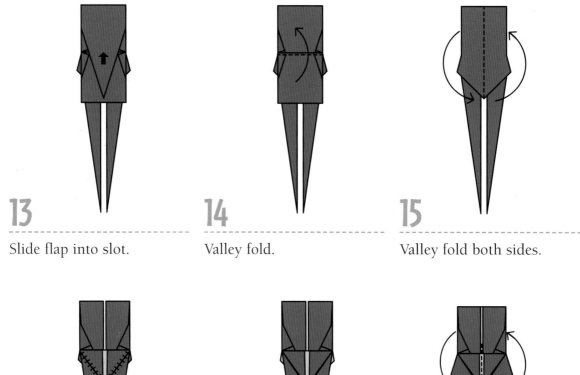

13
Slide flap into slot.

14
Valley fold.

15
Valley fold both sides.

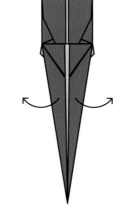

16
Cut top layers, front and back.

17
Valley open cut parts, front and back.

18
Valley fold both sides to open flaps.

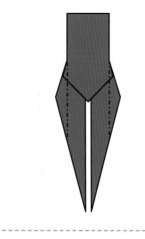

19
Mountain fold top layers.

20
Valley folds.

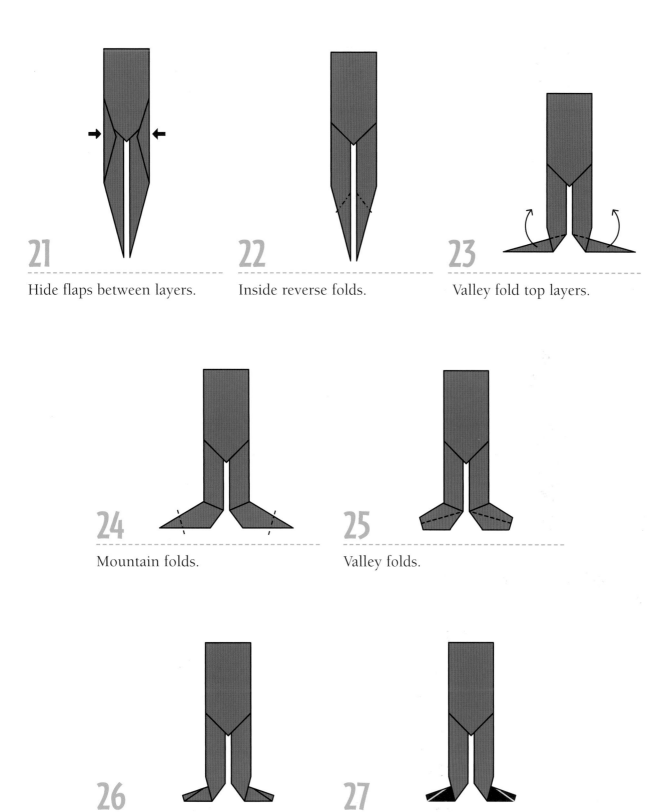

21

Hide flaps between layers.

22

Inside reverse folds.

23

Valley fold top layers.

24

Mountain folds.

25

Valley folds.

26

Add coloring.

27

Completed part 2 of
Frankenstein's monster.

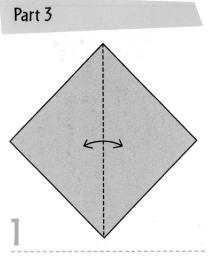

1

Square of paper (2" for 5" body squares, 2.5" for 6" body). Valley fold and unfold.

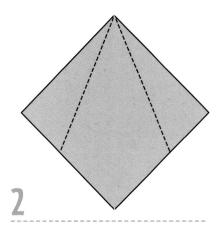

2

Valley folds.

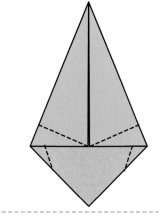

3

Crimp folds.

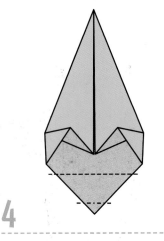

4

Pleat fold.

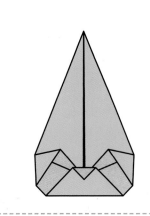

5

Turn over to other side.

6

Valley folds.

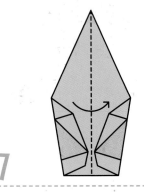

7

Valley fold in half.

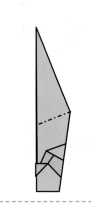

8

Inside reverse fold.

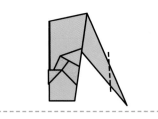

9

Outside reverse fold.

Frankenstein's Monster

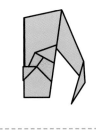

10

Add color to both sides.

11

Open out forward.

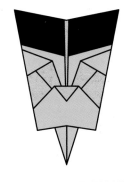

12

Completed part 3 of Frankenstein's monster.

To Attach

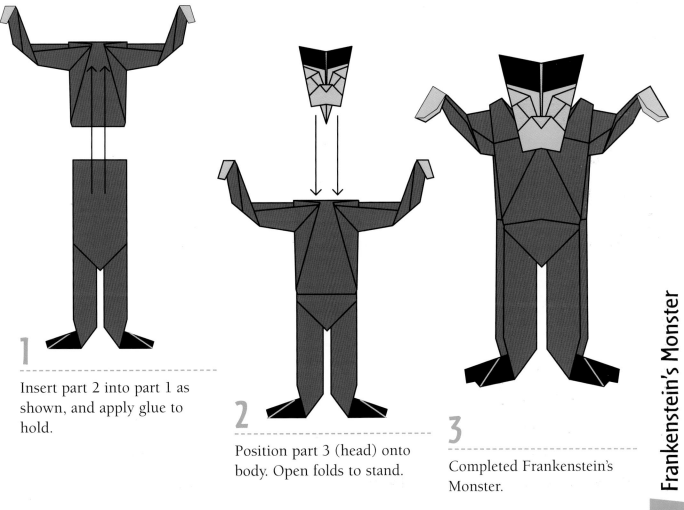

1

Insert part 2 into part 1 as shown, and apply glue to hold.

2

Position part 3 (head) onto body. Open folds to stand.

3

Completed Frankenstein's Monster.

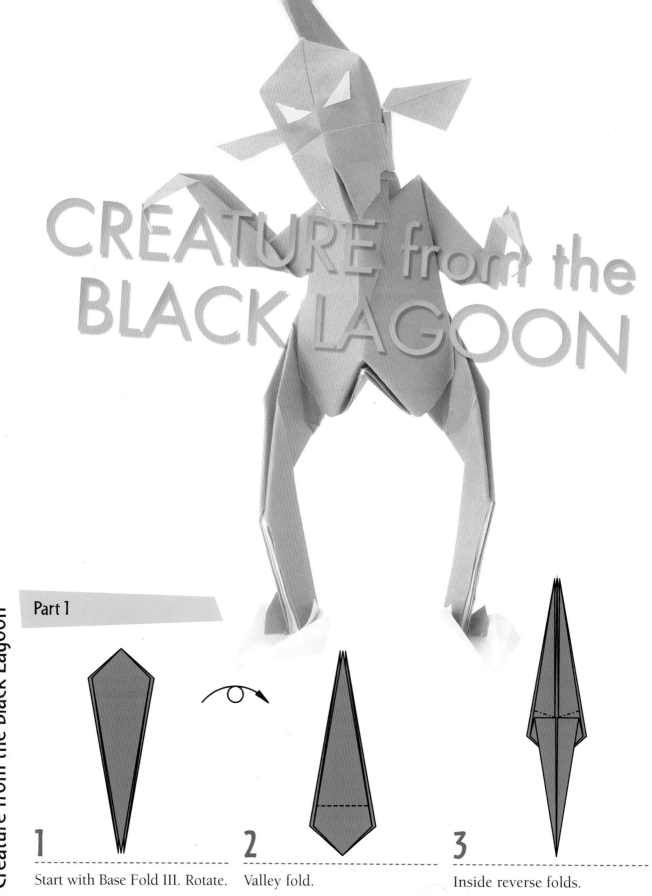

Part 1

1 Start with Base Fold III. Rotate.

2 Valley fold.

3 Inside reverse folds.

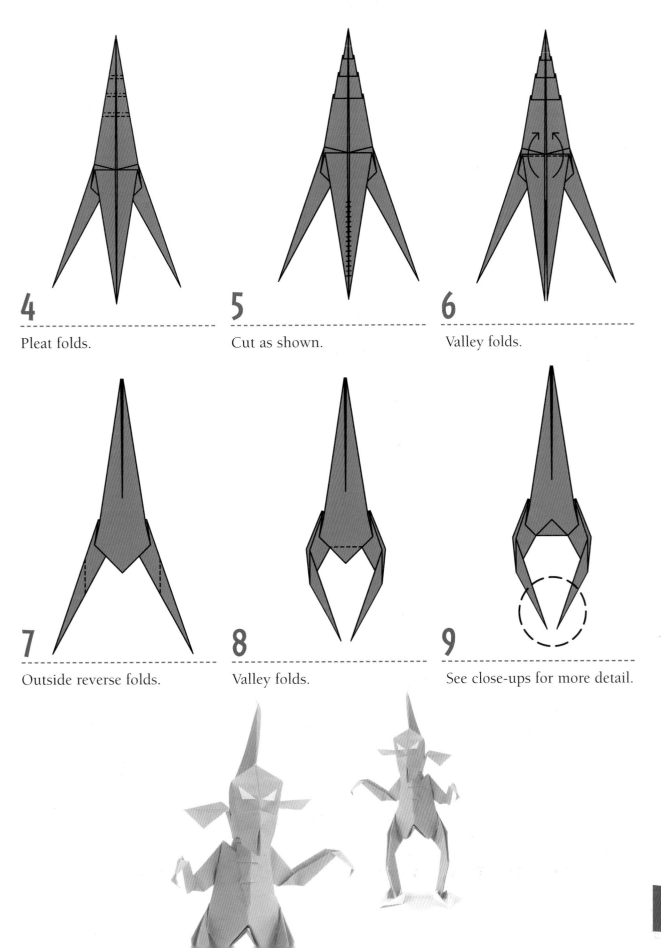

4

Pleat folds.

5

Cut as shown.

6

Valley folds.

7

Outside reverse folds.

8

Valley folds.

9

See close-ups for more detail.

Creature from the Black Lagoon

39

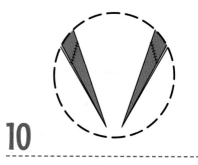

10

Cuts to top layers, front and back.

11

Valley open, front and back.

12

Cuts to top layers, front and back.

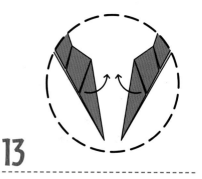

13

Valley open, front and back.

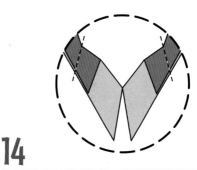

14

Outside reverse folds.

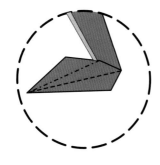

15

Pleat fold right side loosely, front and back.

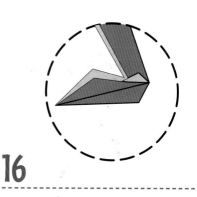

16

Pleat completed.

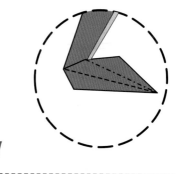

17

Repeat pleat fold on left side, front and back.

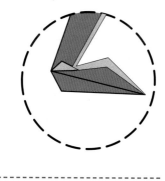

18

Back to full view.

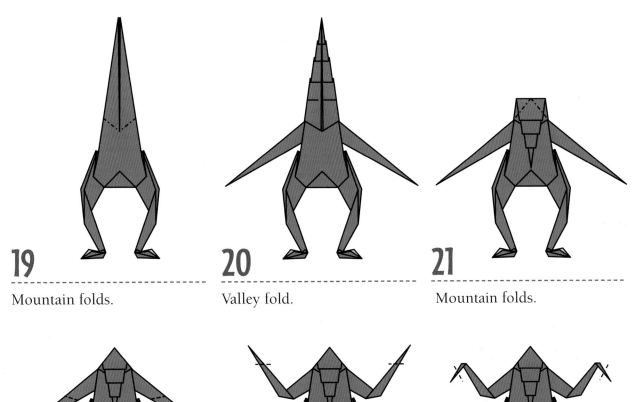

19

Mountain folds.

20

Valley fold.

21

Mountain folds.

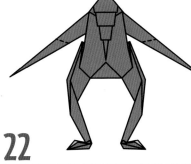

22

Valley folds.

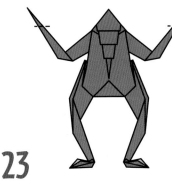

23

Valley folds.

24

Outside reverse folds.

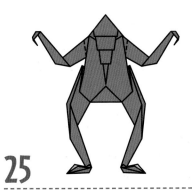

25

Valley folds, to position forward.

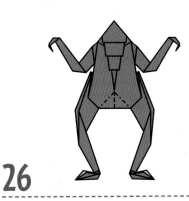

26

Inside reverse folds, to open body.

27

Completed part 1 of creature.

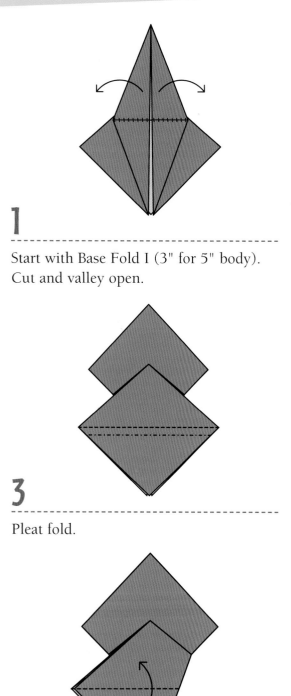

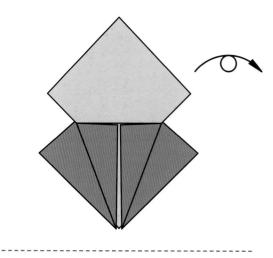

1

Start with Base Fold I (3" for 5" body).
Cut and valley open.

2

Turn over to other side.

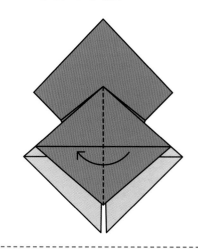

3

Pleat fold.

4

Valley fold.

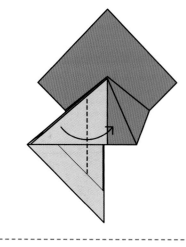

5

Valley fold.

6

Valley fold.

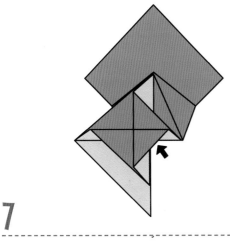

7

Hide flap behind layer.

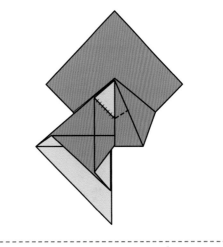

8

Cut as shown and valley fold.

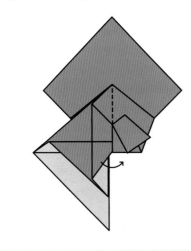

9

Valley fold top layer.

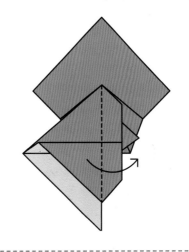

10

Valley fold.

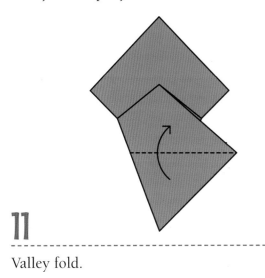

11

Valley fold.

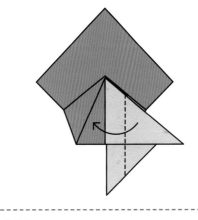

12

Valley fold.

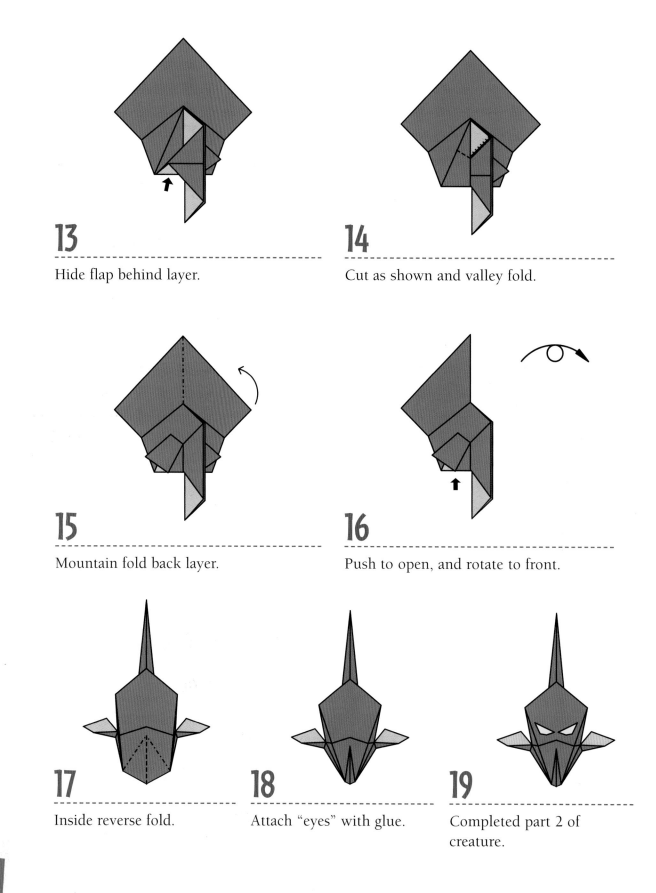

13

Hide flap behind layer.

14

Cut as shown and valley fold.

15

Mountain fold back layer.

16

Push to open, and rotate to front.

17

Inside reverse fold.

18

Attach "eyes" with glue.

19

Completed part 2 of creature.

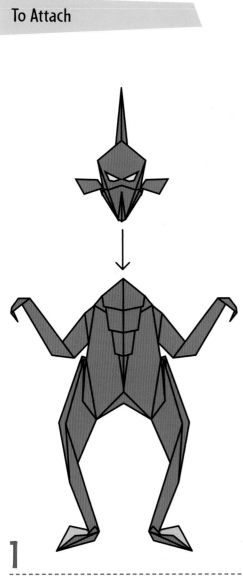

1

Join both parts together as shown and apply glue to hold.

2

Completed Creature from the Black Lagoon.

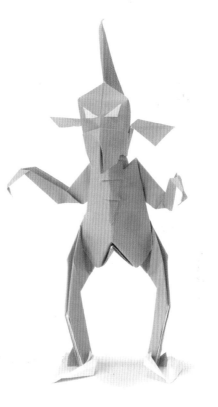

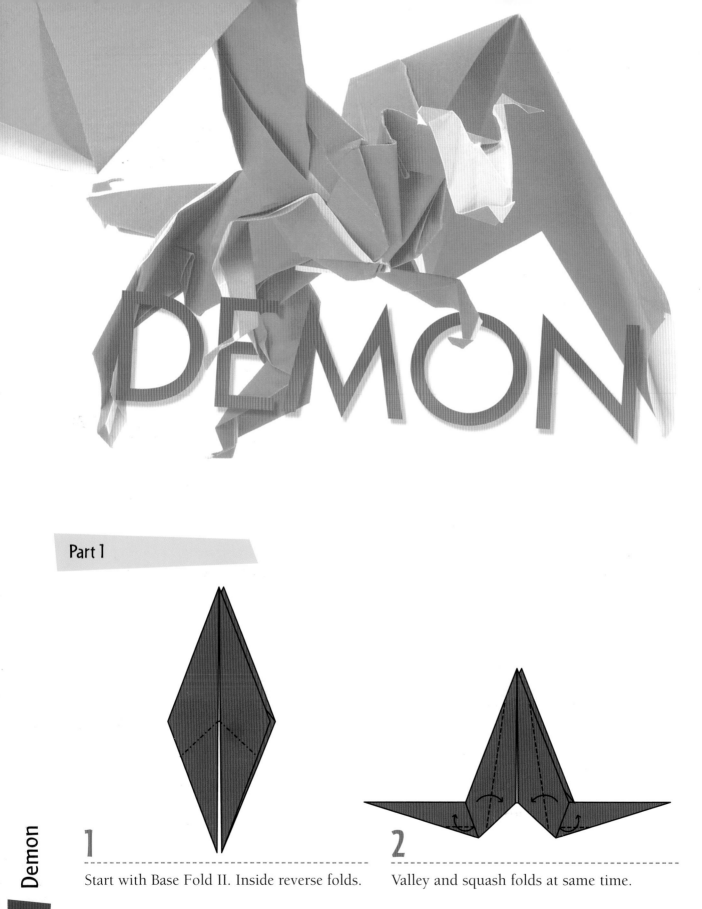

DEMON

Part 1

1

Start with Base Fold II. Inside reverse folds.

2

Valley and squash folds at same time.

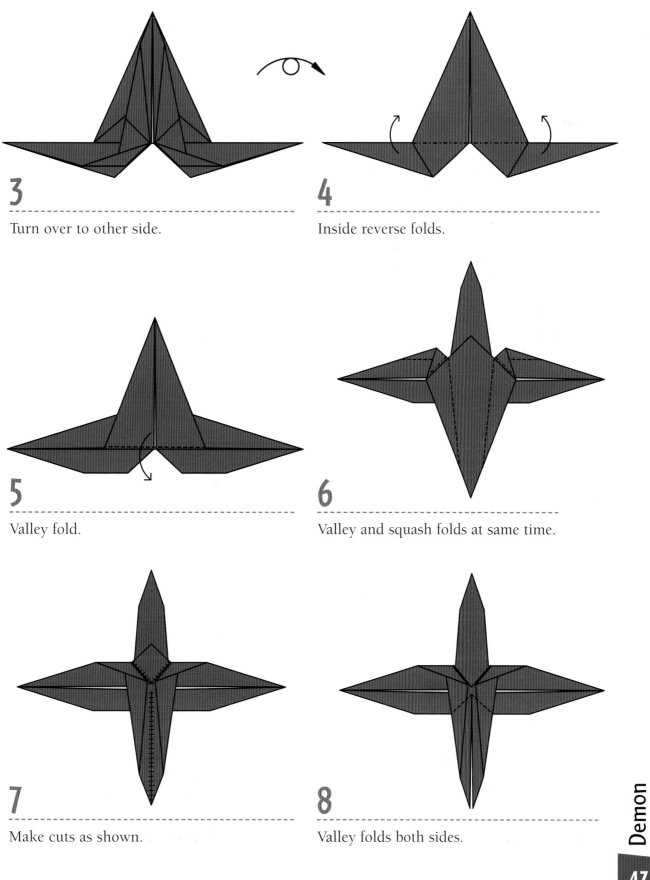

3

Turn over to other side.

4

Inside reverse folds.

5

Valley fold.

6

Valley and squash folds at same time.

7

Make cuts as shown.

8

Valley folds both sides.

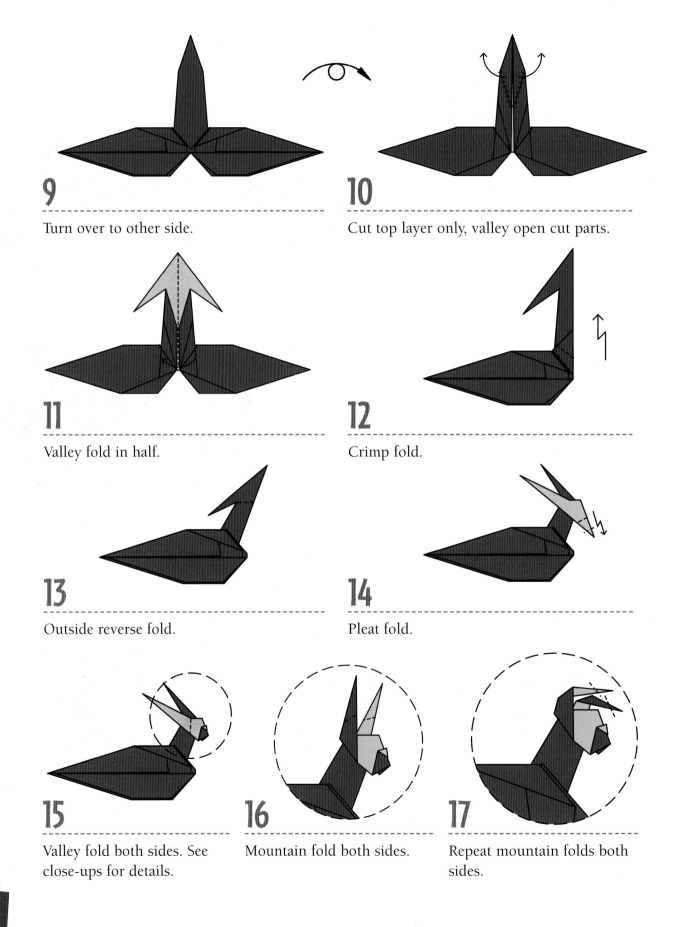

9

Turn over to other side.

10

Cut top layer only, valley open cut parts.

11

Valley fold in half.

12

Crimp fold.

13

Outside reverse fold.

14

Pleat fold.

15

Valley fold both sides. See close-ups for details.

16

Mountain fold both sides.

17

Repeat mountain folds both sides.

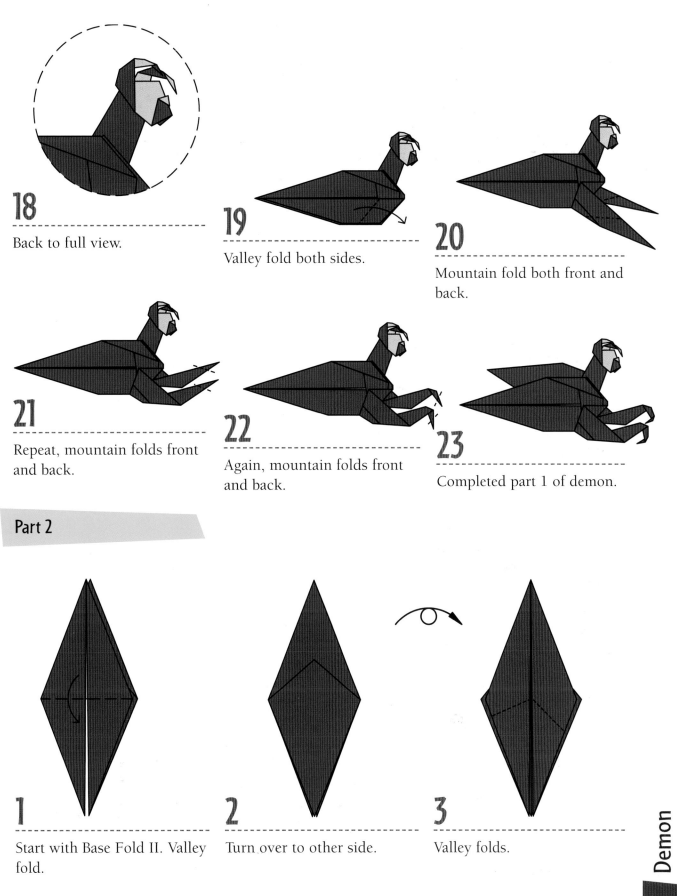

18

Back to full view.

19

Valley fold both sides.

20

Mountain fold both front and back.

21

Repeat, mountain folds front and back.

22

Again, mountain folds front and back.

23

Completed part 1 of demon.

Part 2

1

Start with Base Fold II. Valley fold.

2

Turn over to other side.

3

Valley folds.

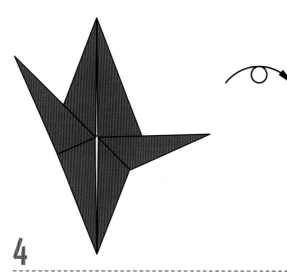

4

Turn over to other side.

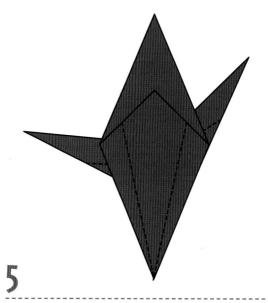

5

Valley and squash fold both sides. Inside reverse folds.

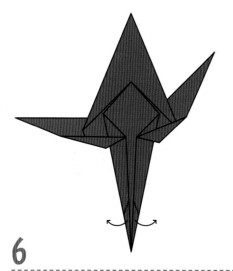

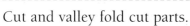

6

Cut and valley fold cut parts.

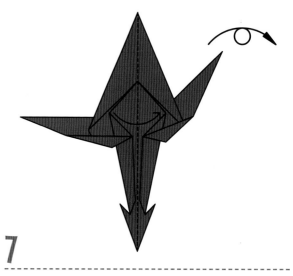

7

Valley fold in half. Rotate.

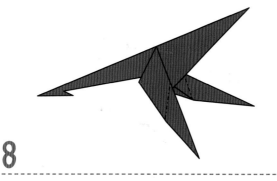

8

Inside reverse folds.

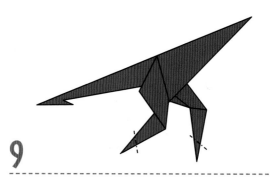

9

Inside reverse folds.

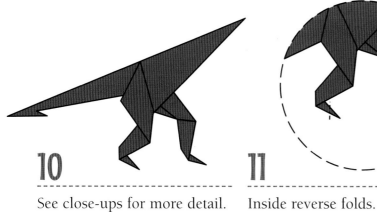

10

See close-ups for more detail.

11

Inside reverse folds.

12

Cut edges to separate. Back to full view.

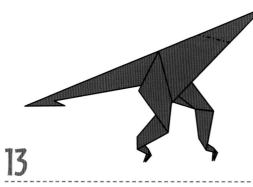

13

Inside reverse fold.

14

Inside reverse fold.

15

Mountain fold.

16

Completed part 2 of demon.

1

Valley fold two squares (3" for 5" body).

2

Rotate one sheet as shown.

3

Insert rotated sheet between layers as shown.

4

Valley fold. (Mountain fold for part 4.)

5

Turn over for part 3 only.

6

Valley fold, allowing back flap to come forward.

7

Valley fold flap.

6

Valley fold, allowing back flap to come forward.

7

Valley fold flap.

8

Open out and rotate forward.

9

Completed part 3 of demon.

8

Open out and rotate forward.

9

Completed part 4 of demon.

Demon

1

Join parts 1 and 2 and apply glue to hold.

2

Insert wings into slots, and secure with glue.

3

Valley fold inner wings, both sides.

4

Completed Demon.

Demon

WEREWOLF

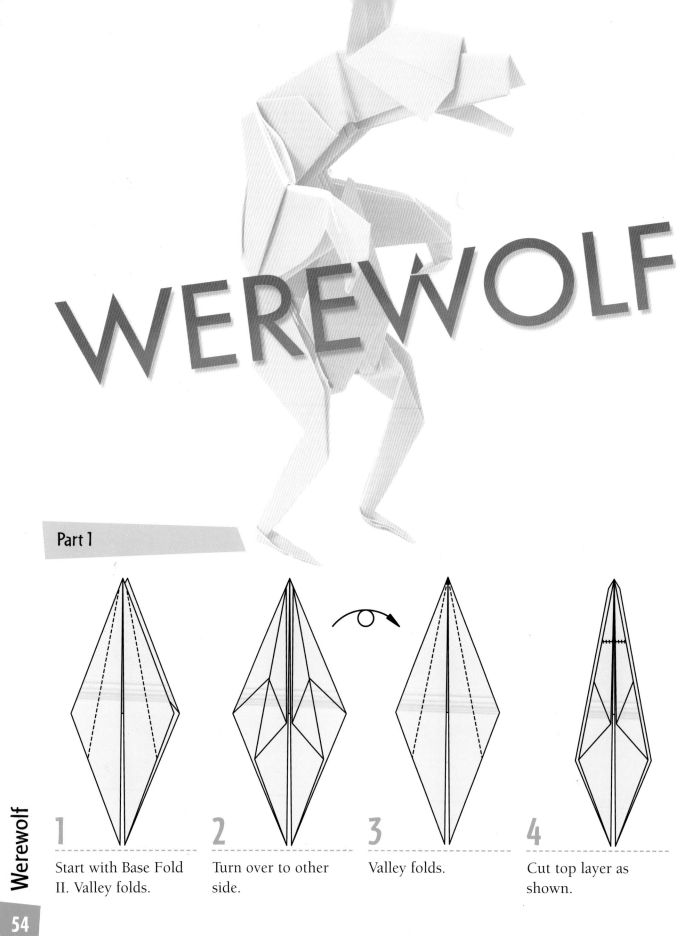

Part 1

1 Start with Base Fold II. Valley folds.

2 Turn over to other side.

3 Valley folds.

4 Cut top layer as shown.

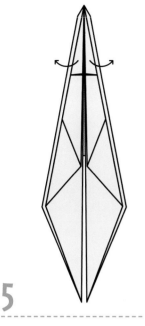

5

Valley open.

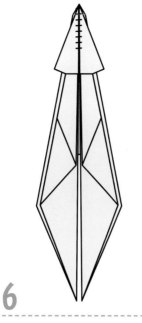

6

Cut the top flap.

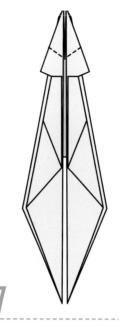

7

Valley folds.

8

Valley folds.

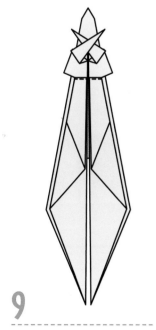

9

Valley folds.

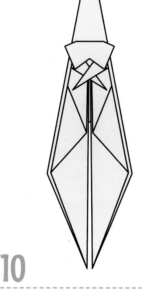

10

Turn over to other side.

11

Pleat fold.

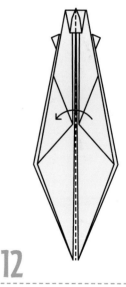

12

Valley fold in half.

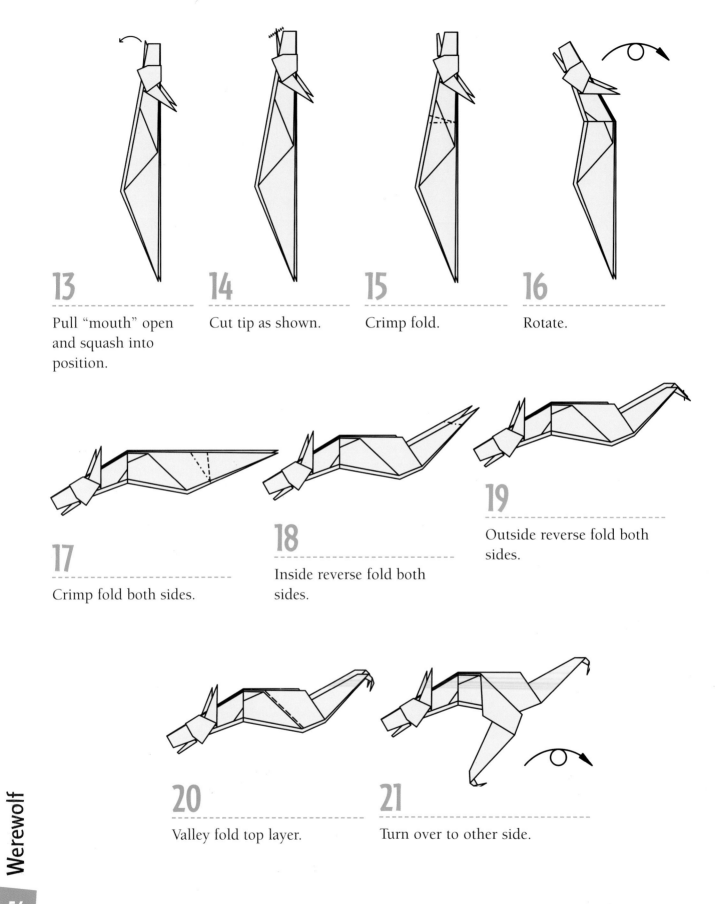

13

Pull "mouth" open and squash into position.

14

Cut tip as shown.

15

Crimp fold.

16

Rotate.

17

Crimp fold both sides.

18

Inside reverse fold both sides.

19

Outside reverse fold both sides.

20

Valley fold top layer.

21

Turn over to other side.

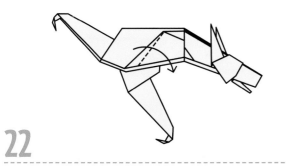

22

Valley fold top layer.

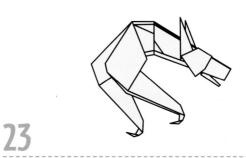

23

Completed part 1 of werewolf.

Part 2

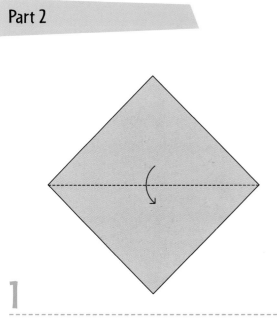

1

Valley fold square (same size as Part 1) in half.

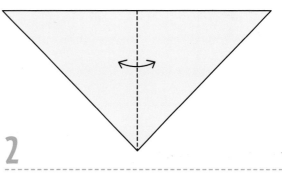

2

Valley fold and unfold.

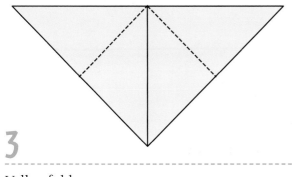

3

Valley folds.

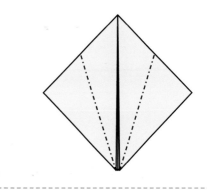

4

Inside reverse folds.

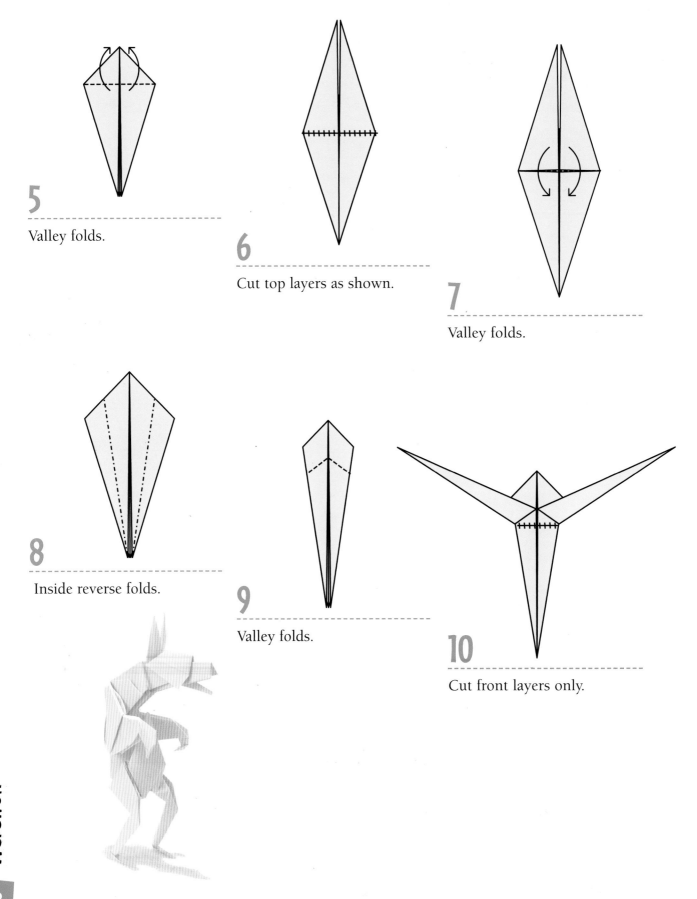

5

Valley folds.

6

Cut top layers as shown.

7

Valley folds.

8

Inside reverse folds.

9

Valley folds.

10

Cut front layers only.

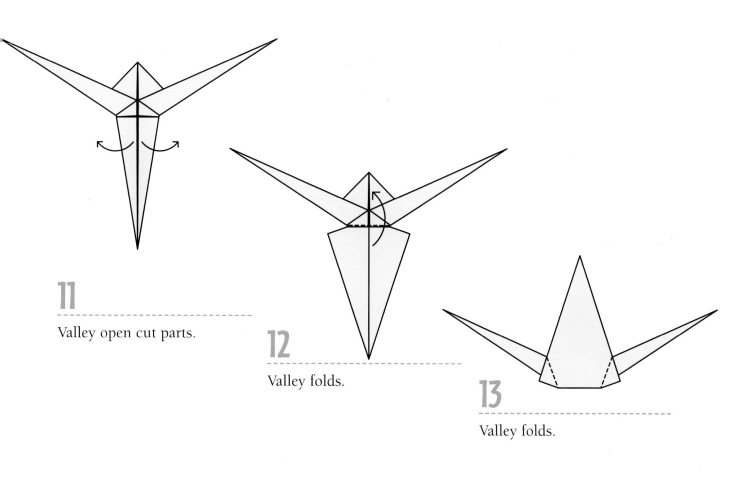

11
Valley open cut parts.

12
Valley folds.

13
Valley folds.

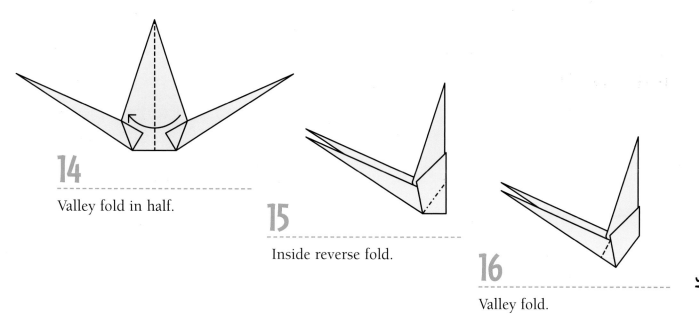

14
Valley fold in half.

15
Inside reverse fold.

16
Valley fold.

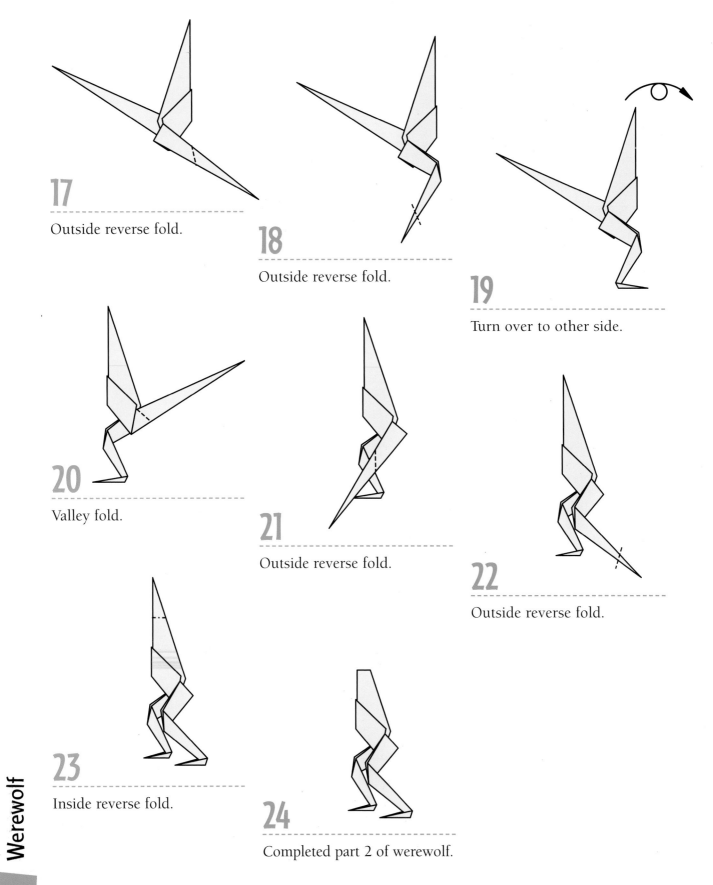

17

Outside reverse fold.

18

Outside reverse fold.

19

Turn over to other side.

20

Valley fold.

21

Outside reverse fold.

22

Outside reverse fold.

23

Inside reverse fold.

24

Completed part 2 of werewolf.

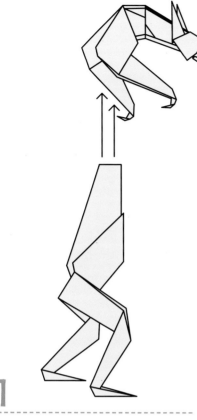

1

Join both parts together as
shown and apply glue
to hold.

2

Completed Werewolf.

WOLFMAN

Wolfman

1

Start with Base Fold II. Inside reverse folds.

2

Valley folds.

3

Turn over to other side.

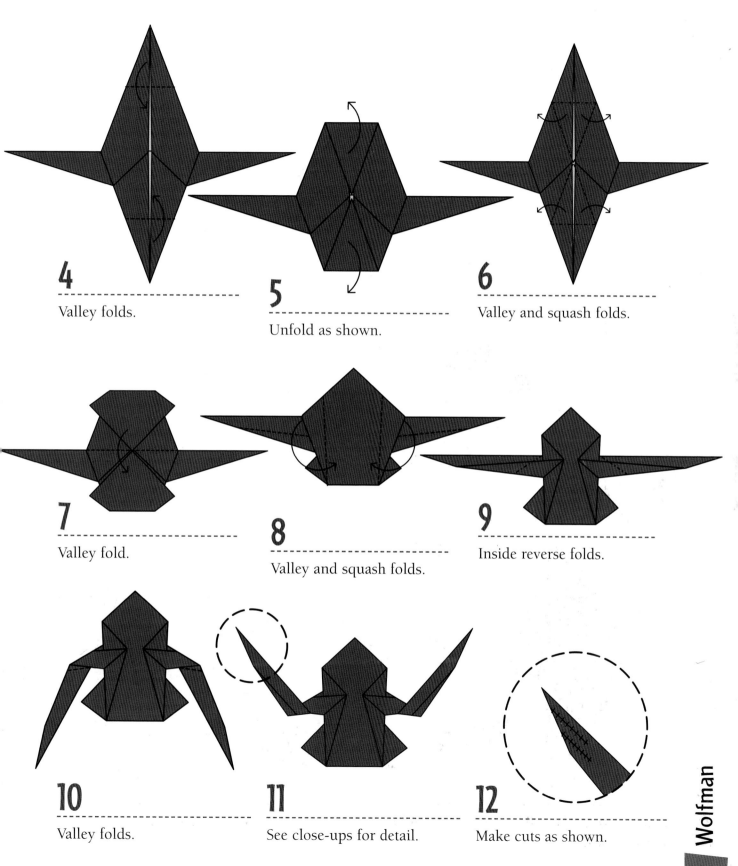

4

Valley folds.

5

Unfold as shown.

6

Valley and squash folds.

7

Valley fold.

8

Valley and squash folds.

9

Inside reverse folds.

10

Valley folds.

11

See close-ups for detail.

12

Make cuts as shown.

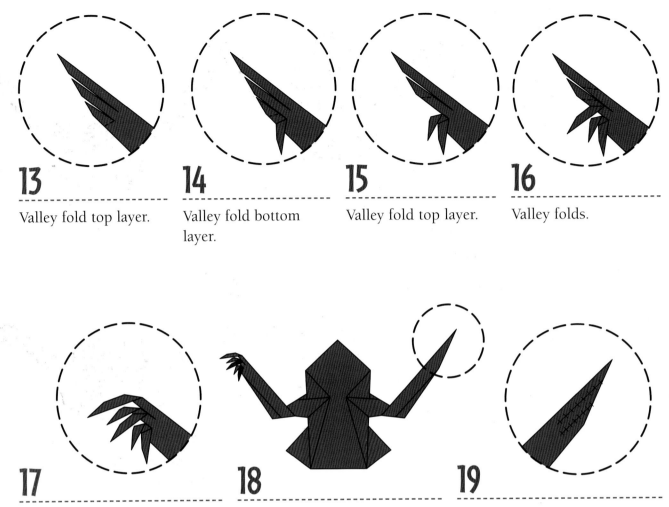

13

Valley fold top layer.

14

Valley fold bottom layer.

15

Valley fold top layer.

16

Valley folds.

17

Back to full view.

18

See close-ups for detail.

19

Make cuts as shown.

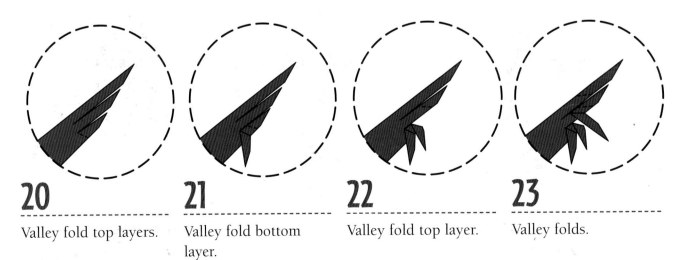

20

Valley fold top layers.

21

Valley fold bottom layer.

22

Valley fold top layer.

23

Valley folds.

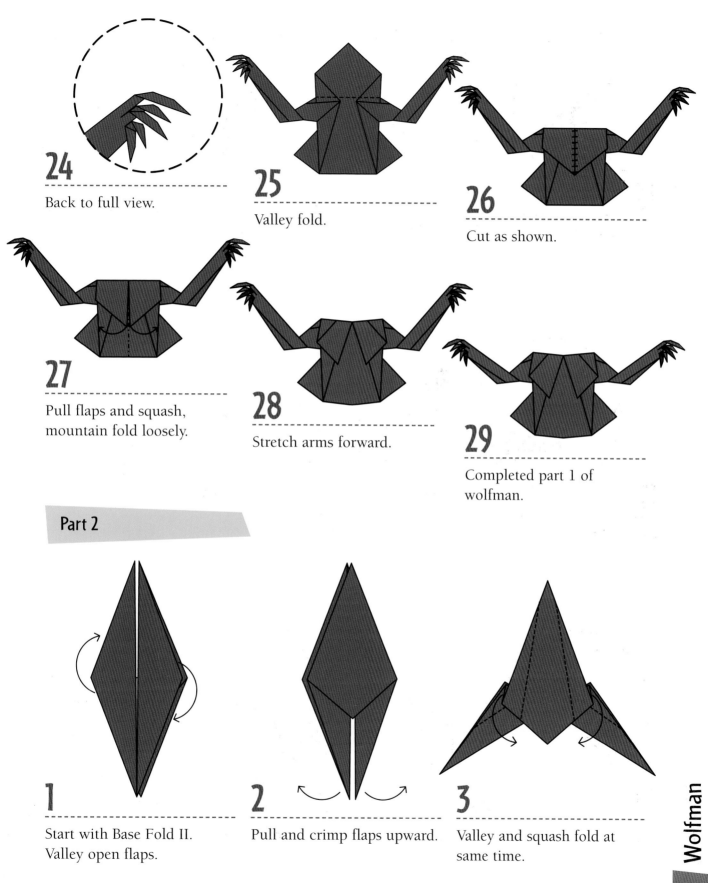

24
Back to full view.

25
Valley fold.

26
Cut as shown.

27
Pull flaps and squash, mountain fold loosely.

28
Stretch arms forward.

29
Completed part 1 of wolfman.

Part 2

1
Start with Base Fold II. Valley open flaps.

2
Pull and crimp flaps upward.

3
Valley and squash fold at same time.

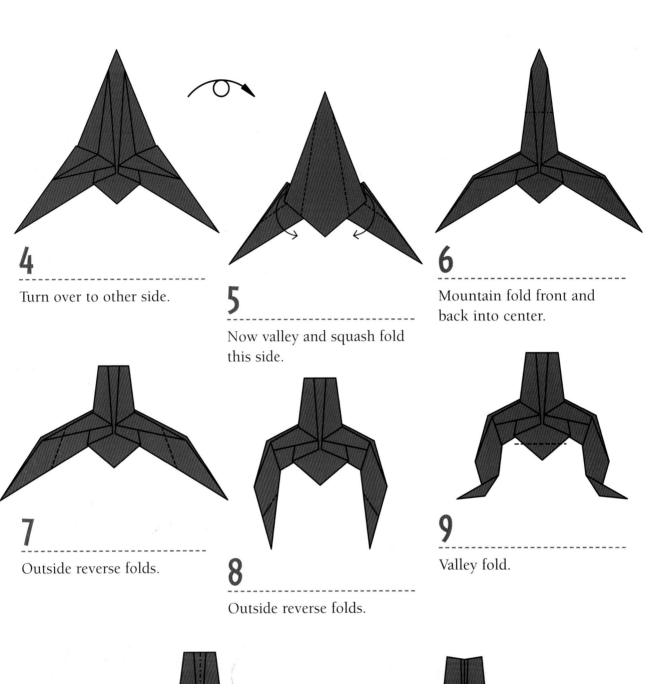

4

Turn over to other side.

5

Now valley and squash fold this side.

6

Mountain fold front and back into center.

7

Outside reverse folds.

8

Outside reverse folds.

9

Valley fold.

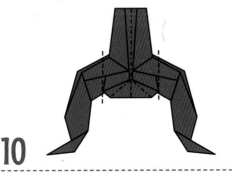

10

Inside reverse center (slightly mountain fold in half), valley folds.

11

Completed part 2 of wolfman.

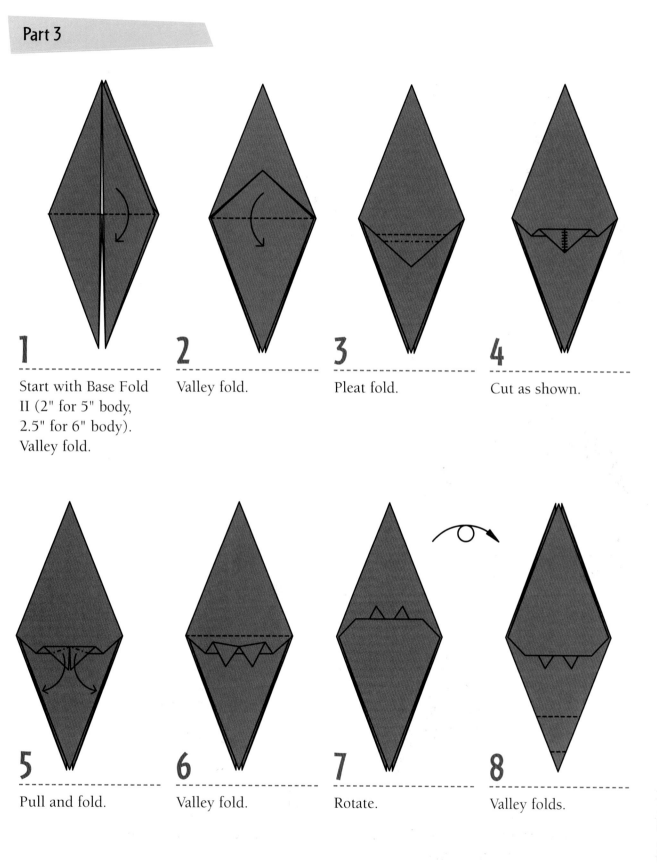

1

Start with Base Fold II (2" for 5" body, 2.5" for 6" body). Valley fold.

2

Valley fold.

3

Pleat fold.

4

Cut as shown.

5

Pull and fold.

6

Valley fold.

7

Rotate.

8

Valley folds.

Wolfman

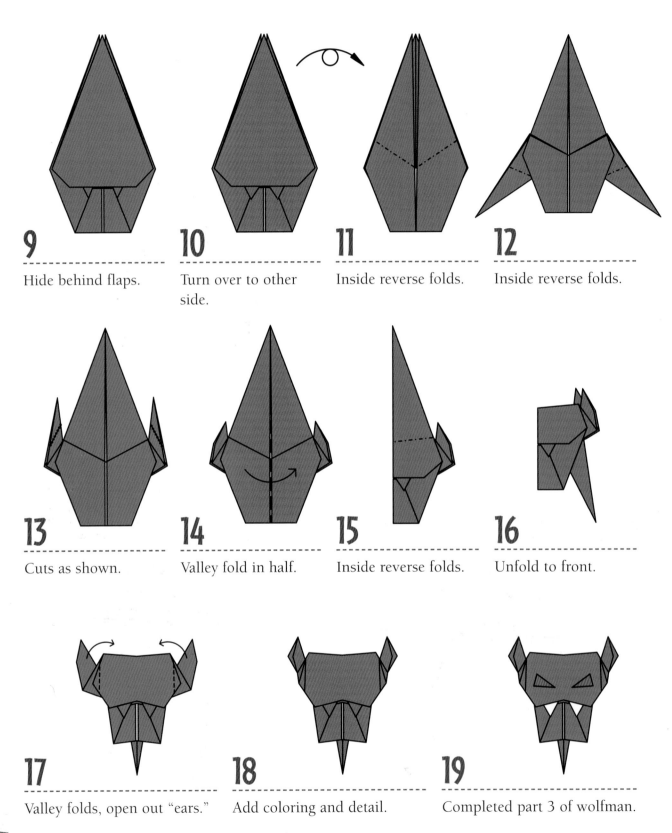

9

Hide behind flaps.

10

Turn over to other side.

11

Inside reverse folds.

12

Inside reverse folds.

13

Cuts as shown.

14

Valley fold in half.

15

Inside reverse folds.

16

Unfold to front.

17

Valley folds, open out "ears."

18

Add coloring and detail.

19

Completed part 3 of wolfman.

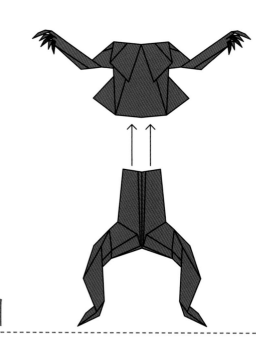

1

Join parts 1 and 2 as shown and apply glue to hold.

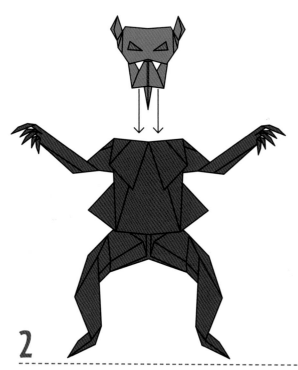

2

Position part 3 and glue between "shoulderblades."

3

Completed Wolfman.

Wolfman

69

KING GHIDORA

Part 1

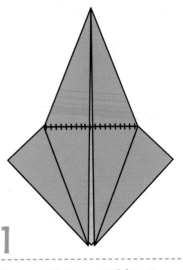

1
Start with Base Fold I. Cuts as shown.

2
Valley fold.

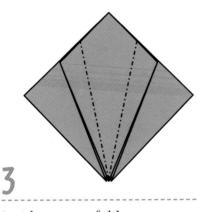

3
Inside reverse folds.

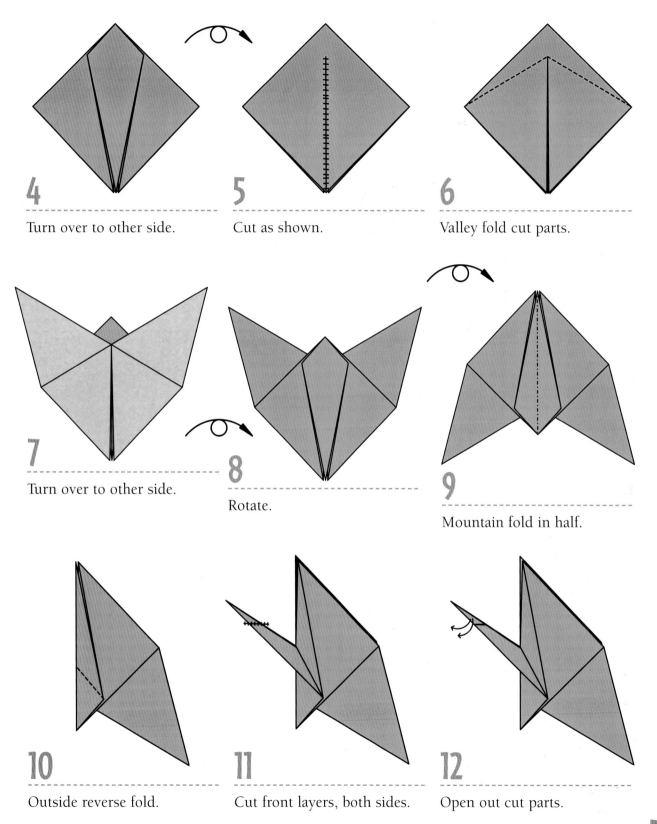

4 Turn over to other side.

5 Cut as shown.

6 Valley fold cut parts.

7 Turn over to other side.

8 Rotate.

9 Mountain fold in half.

10 Outside reverse fold.

11 Cut front layers, both sides.

12 Open out cut parts.

King Ghidora

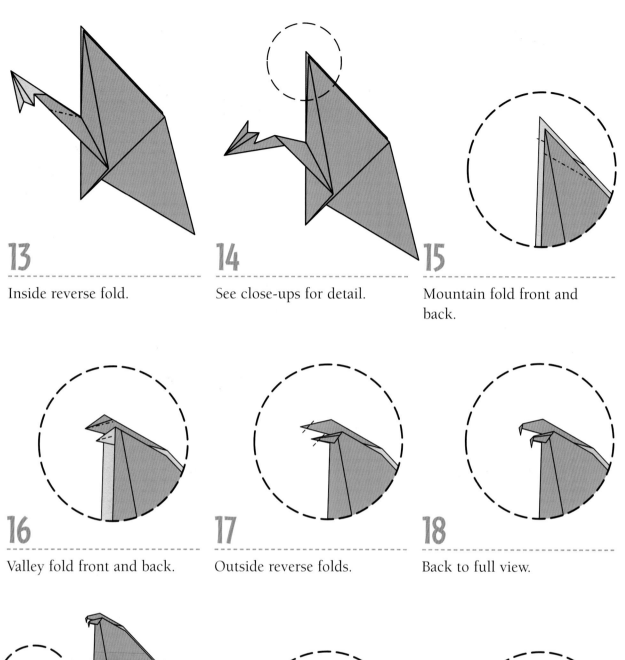

13

Inside reverse fold.

14

See close-ups for detail.

15

Mountain fold front and back.

16

Valley fold front and back.

17

Outside reverse folds.

18

Back to full view.

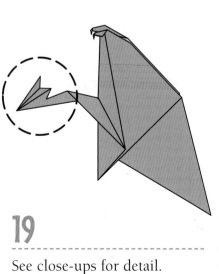

19

See close-ups for detail.

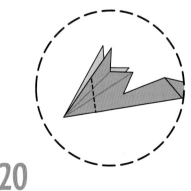

20

Outside reverse folds.

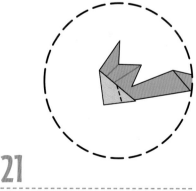

21

Outside reverse folds.

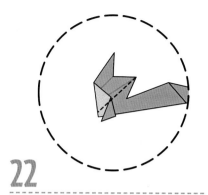

22

Valley fold both sides.

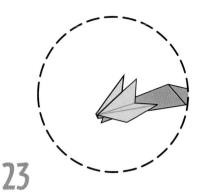

23

Back to full view.

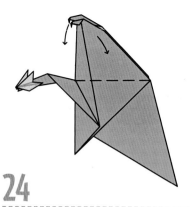

24

Valley fold outward, both sides.

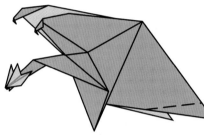

25

Valley folds, front and back.

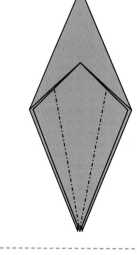

26

Completed part 1 of King Ghidora.

Part 2

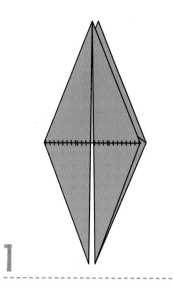

1

Start with Base Fold II. Cut front layers only as shown.

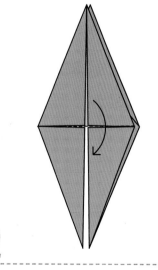

2

Valley fold.

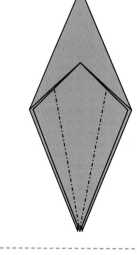

3

Inside reverse folds.

King Ghidora

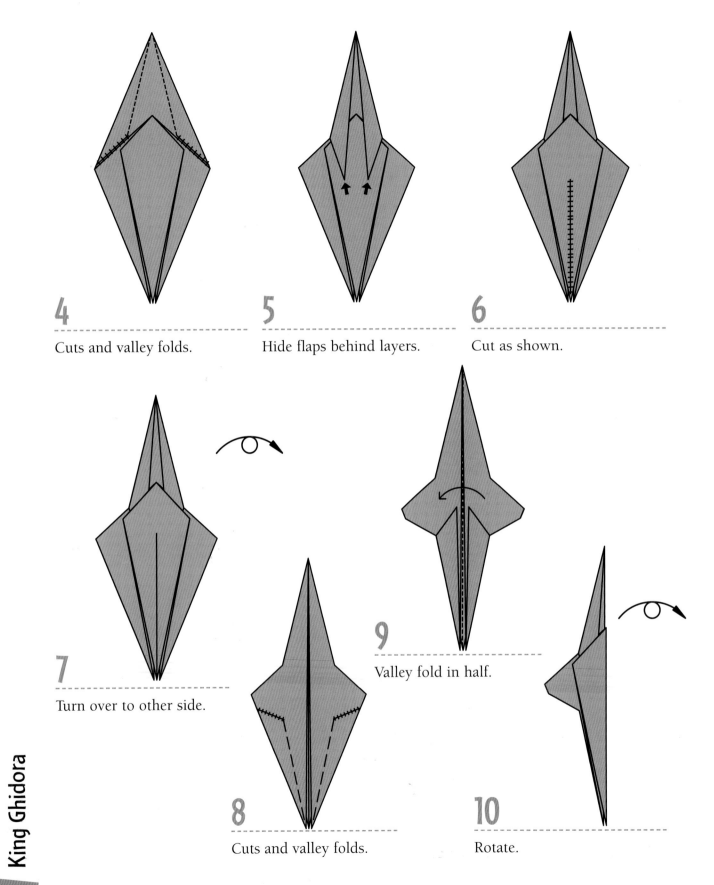

4

Cuts and valley folds.

5

Hide flaps behind layers.

6

Cut as shown.

7

Turn over to other side.

8

Cuts and valley folds.

9

Valley fold in half.

10

Rotate.

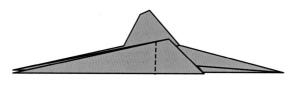

11

Valley fold both front and back.

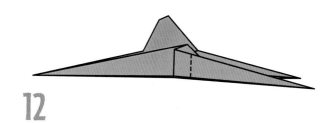

12

Valley fold both front and back.

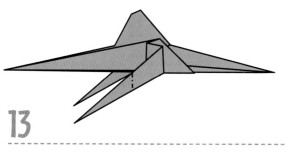

13

Inside reverse fold both sides.

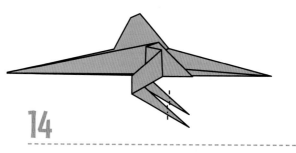

14

Repeat.

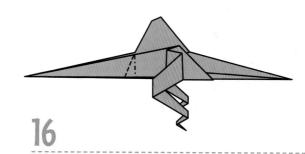

15

Repeat.

16

Crimp fold both sides.

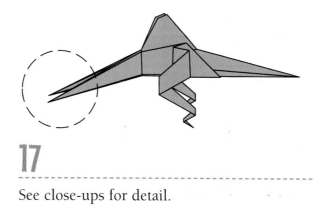

17

See close-ups for detail.

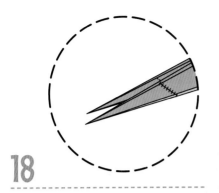

18

Cuts to all four sides.

19

Open out cut parts.

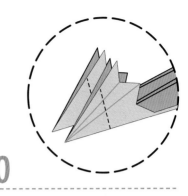

20

Outside reverse folds.

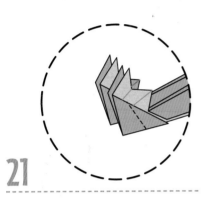

21

Repeat outside reverse folds.

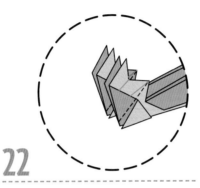

22

Valley fold all sides.

23

Back to full view.

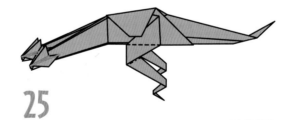

25

Hide flaps, and pleat fold loosely to position "legs."

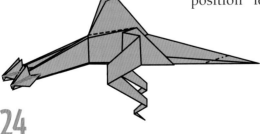

24

Inside reverse fold tail and valley folds to both sides.

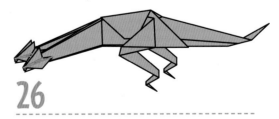

26

Completed part 2 of King Ghidora.

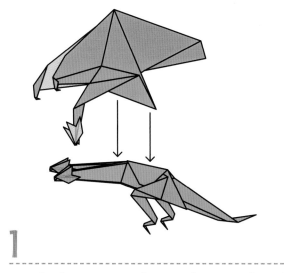

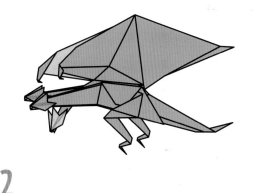

1

Join both parts together as shown and apply glue to hold.

2

Valley fold heads aside to separate.

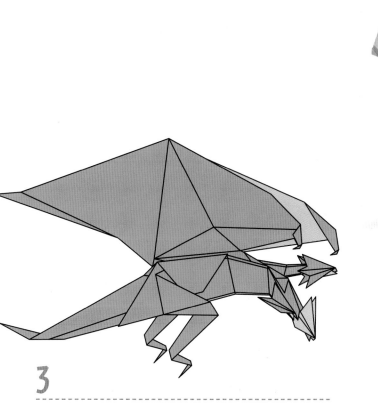

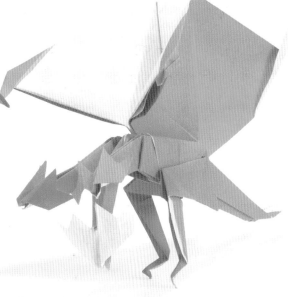

3

Completed King Ghidora.

King Ghidora

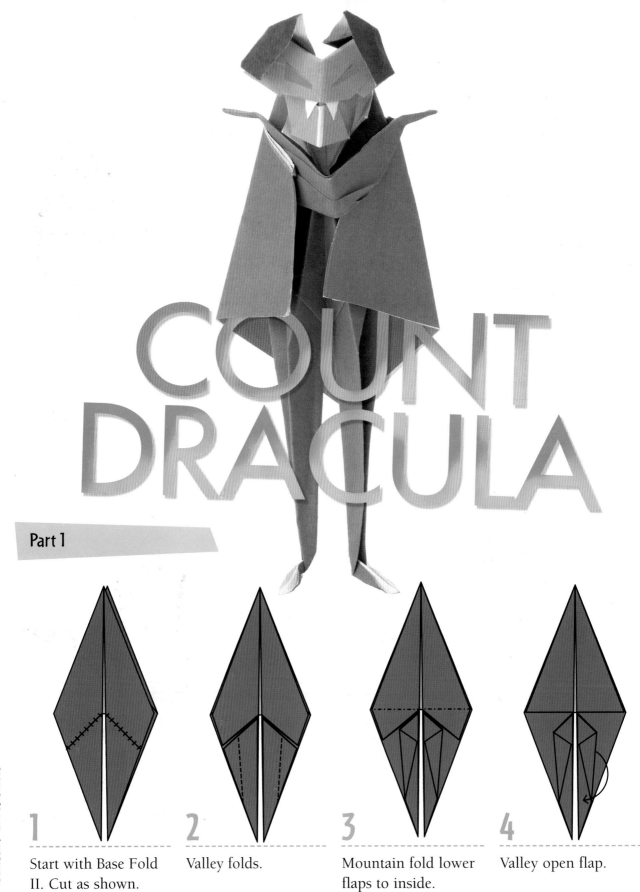

COUNT
DRACULA

Part 1

1 Start with Base Fold II. Cut as shown.

2 Valley folds.

3 Mountain fold lower flaps to inside.

4 Valley open flap.

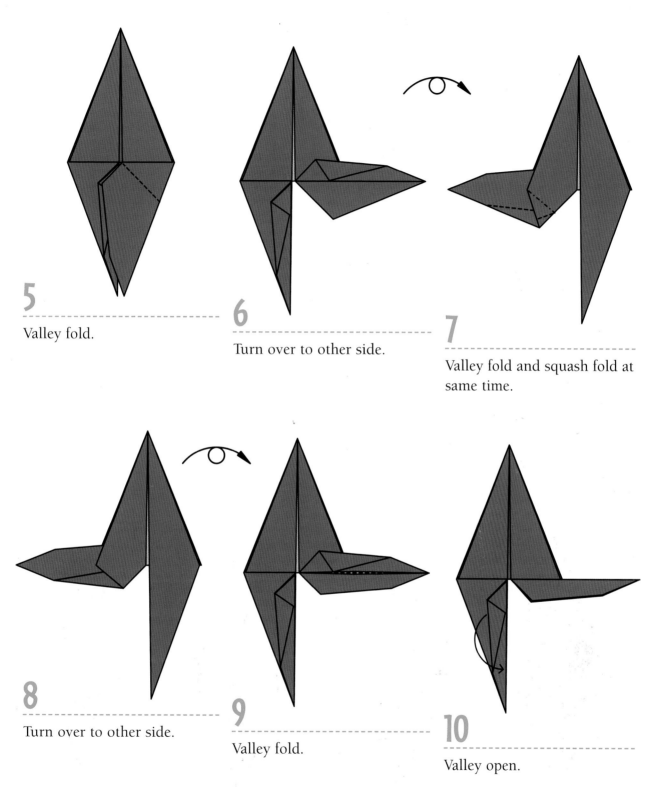

5

Valley fold.

6

Turn over to other side.

7

Valley fold and squash fold at same time.

8

Turn over to other side.

9

Valley fold.

10

Valley open.

Count Dracula

79

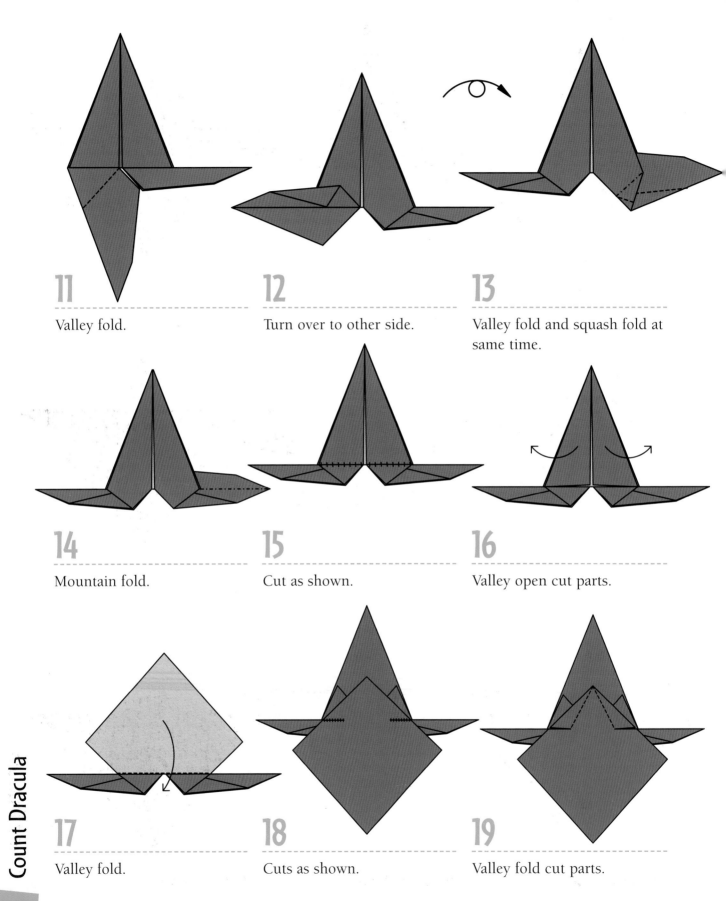

11

Valley fold.

12

Turn over to other side.

13

Valley fold and squash fold at same time.

14

Mountain fold.

15

Cut as shown.

16

Valley open cut parts.

17

Valley fold.

18

Cuts as shown.

19

Valley fold cut parts.

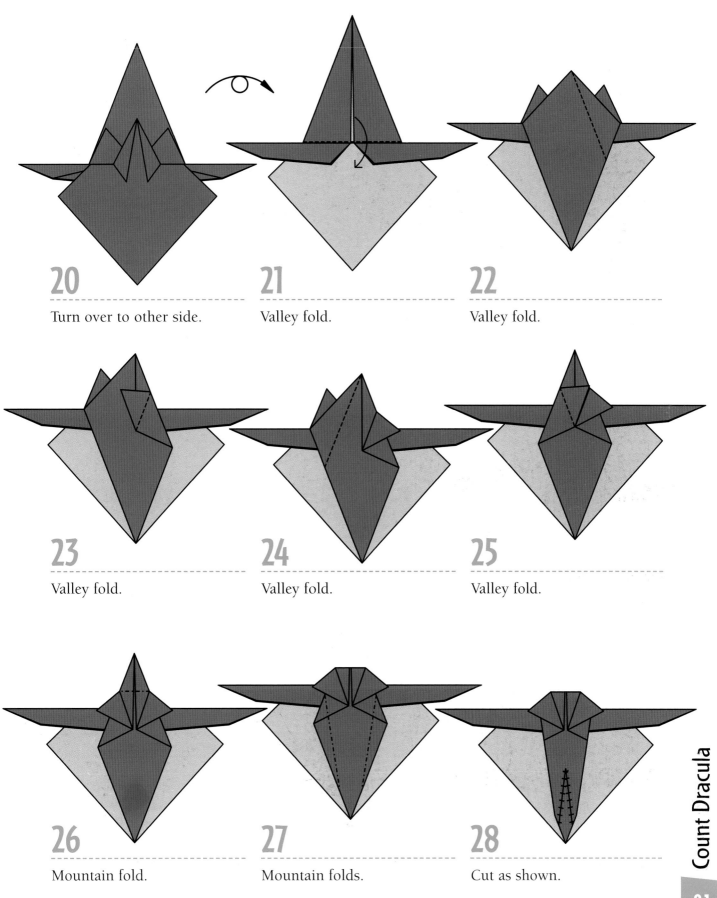

20

Turn over to other side.

21

Valley fold.

22

Valley fold.

23

Valley fold.

24

Valley fold.

25

Valley fold.

26

Mountain fold.

27

Mountain folds.

28

Cut as shown.

Count Dracula

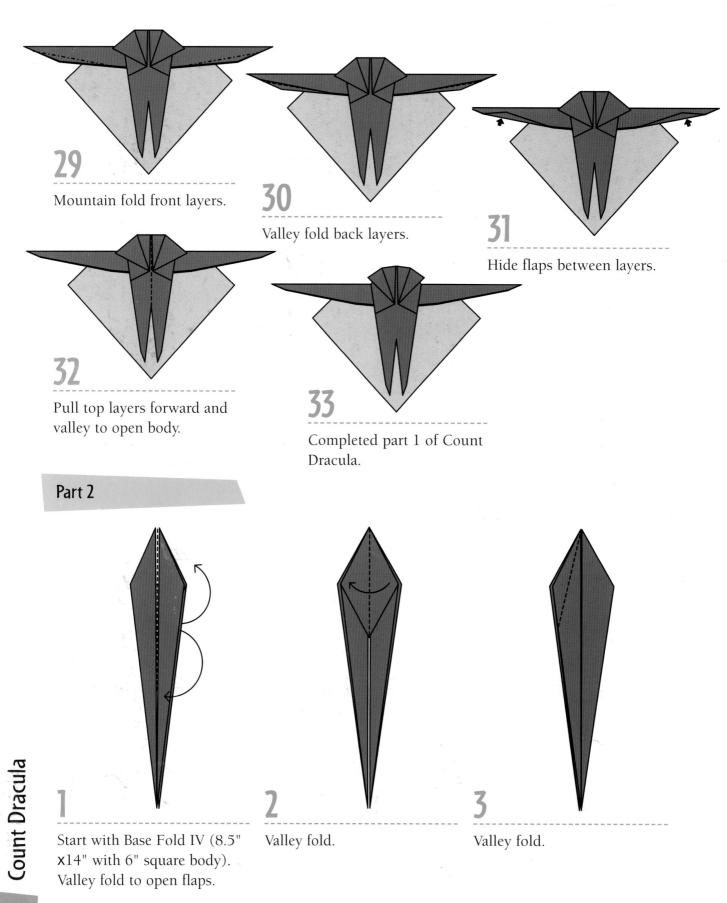

29 Mountain fold front layers.

30 Valley fold back layers.

31 Hide flaps between layers.

32 Pull top layers forward and valley to open body.

33 Completed part 1 of Count Dracula.

Part 2

1 Start with Base Fold IV (8.5" x14" with 6" square body). Valley fold to open flaps.

2 Valley fold.

3 Valley fold.

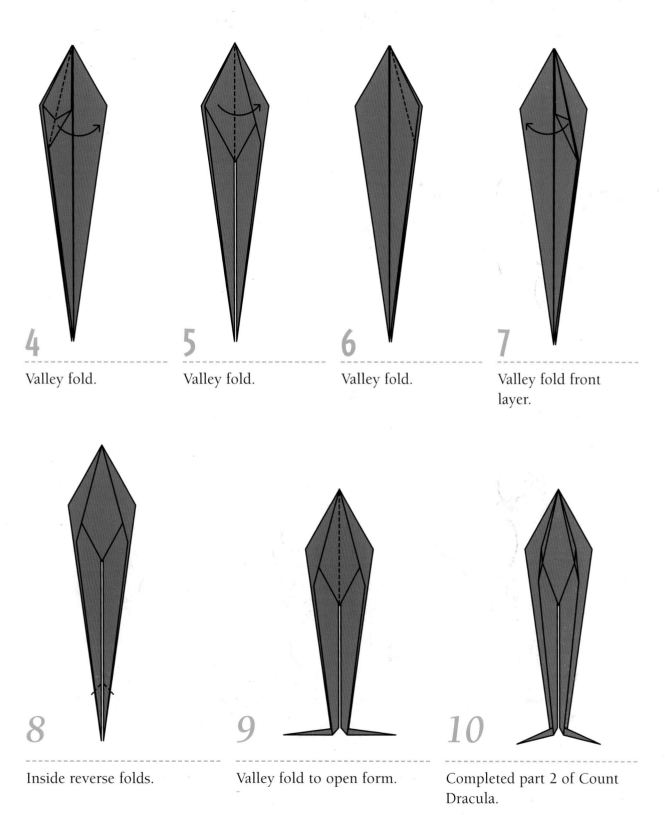

4
Valley fold.

5
Valley fold.

6
Valley fold.

7
Valley fold front layer.

8
Inside reverse folds.

9
Valley fold to open form.

10
Completed part 2 of Count Dracula.

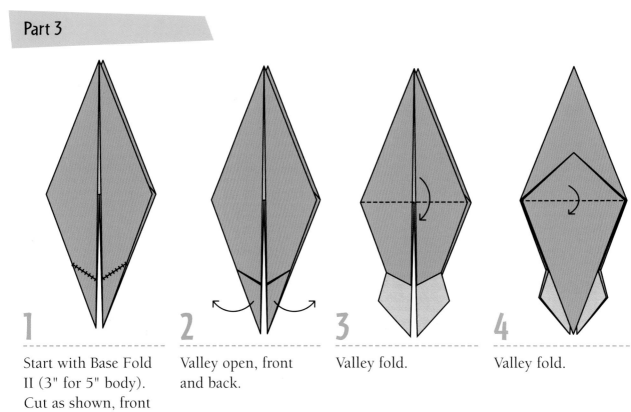

1

Start with Base Fold II (3" for 5" body). Cut as shown, front and back.

2

Valley open, front and back.

3

Valley fold.

4

Valley fold.

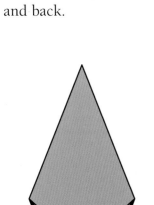
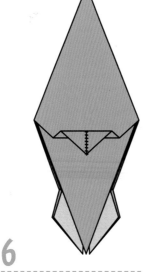
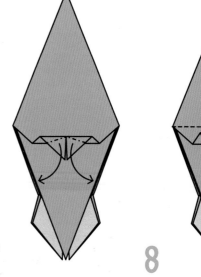
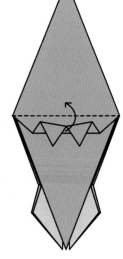

5

Pleat fold.

6

Cut as shown.

7

Pull open and squash fold.

8

Valley fold.

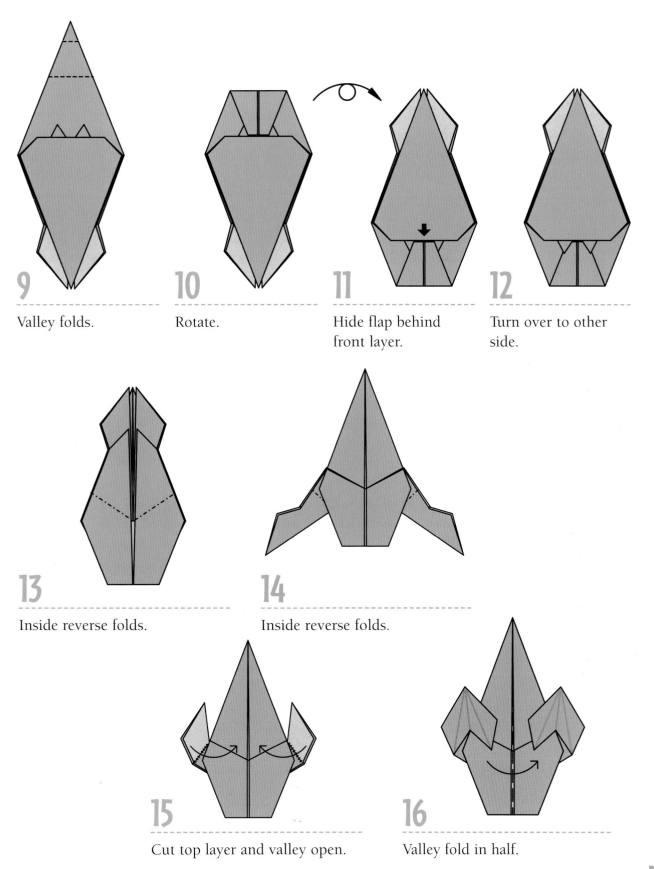

9

Valley folds.

10

Rotate.

11

Hide flap behind
front layer.

12

Turn over to other
side.

13

Inside reverse folds.

14

Inside reverse folds.

15

Cut top layer and valley open.

16

Valley fold in half.

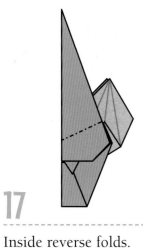

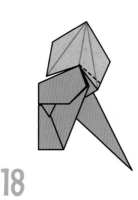

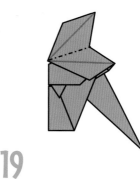

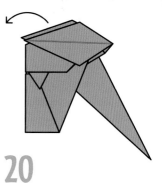

17
Inside reverse folds.

18
Valley fold.

19
Mountain fold.

20
Open out and turn forward.

21
Add coloring and detail.

22
Completed part 3 of Count Dracula.

To Attach

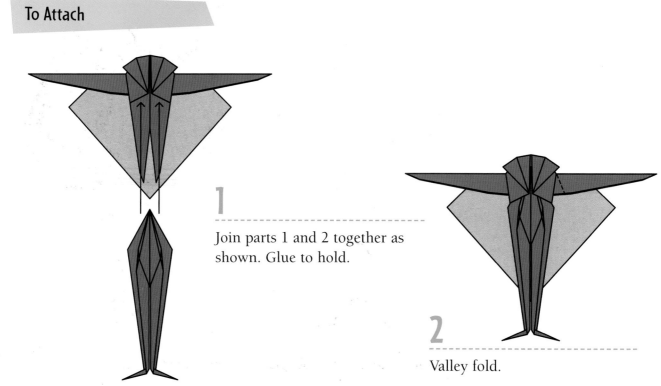

1
Join parts 1 and 2 together as shown. Glue to hold.

2
Valley fold.

Count Dracula

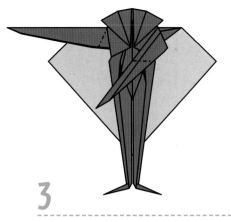

3

Mountain fold.

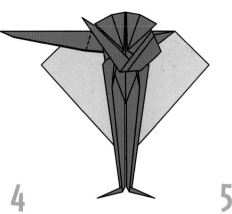

4

Repeat steps 2 and 3 on other side.

5

Valley folds.

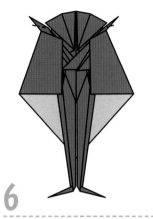

6

Mountain folds, and add detail and coloring

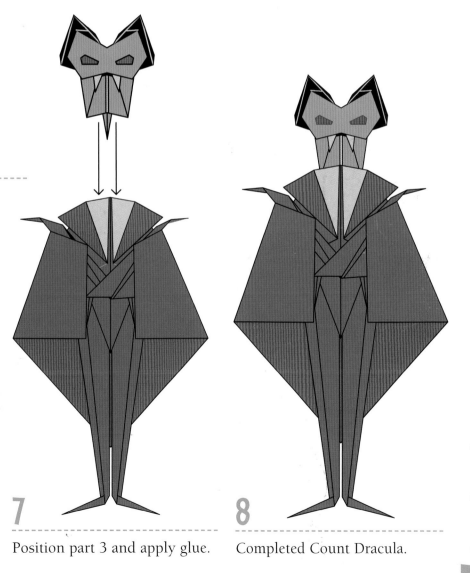

7

Position part 3 and apply glue.

8

Completed Count Dracula.

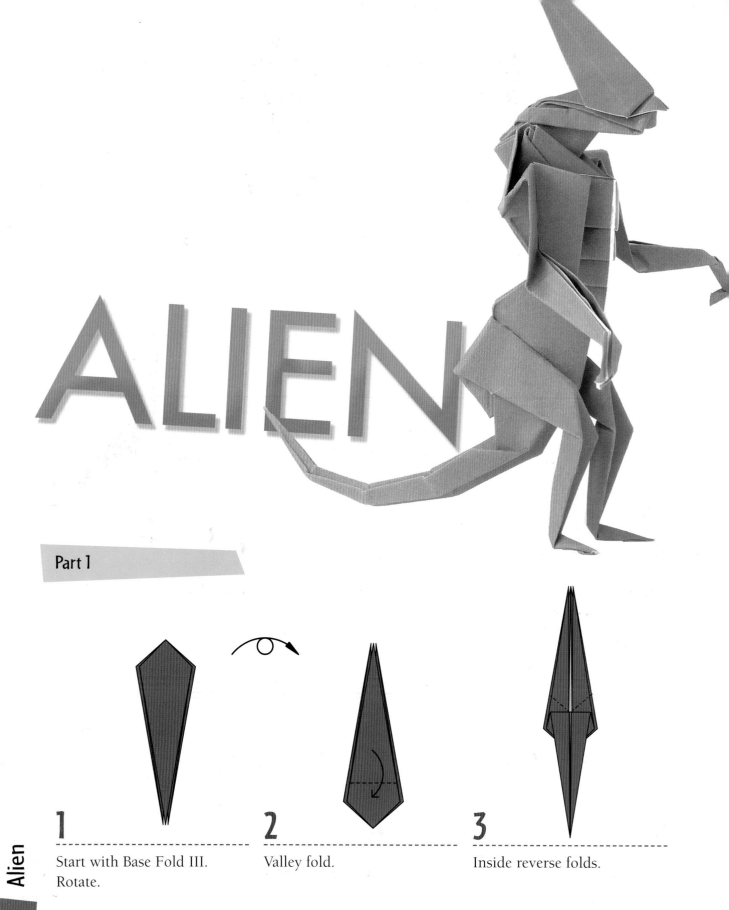

ALIEN

Part 1

1
Start with Base Fold III.
Rotate.

2
Valley fold.

3
Inside reverse folds.

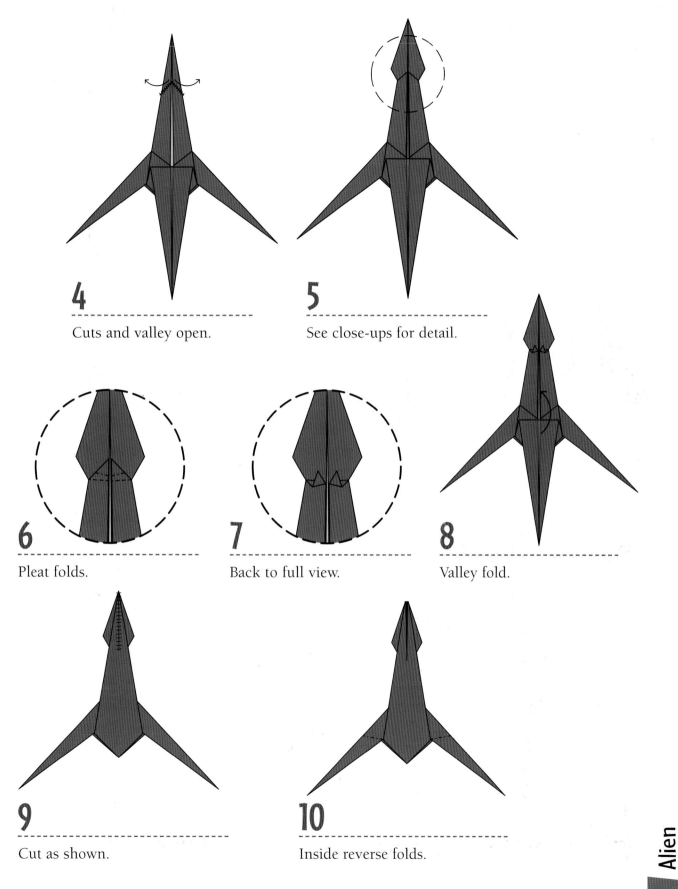

4

Cuts and valley open.

5

See close-ups for detail.

6

Pleat folds.

7

Back to full view.

8

Valley fold.

9

Cut as shown.

10

Inside reverse folds.

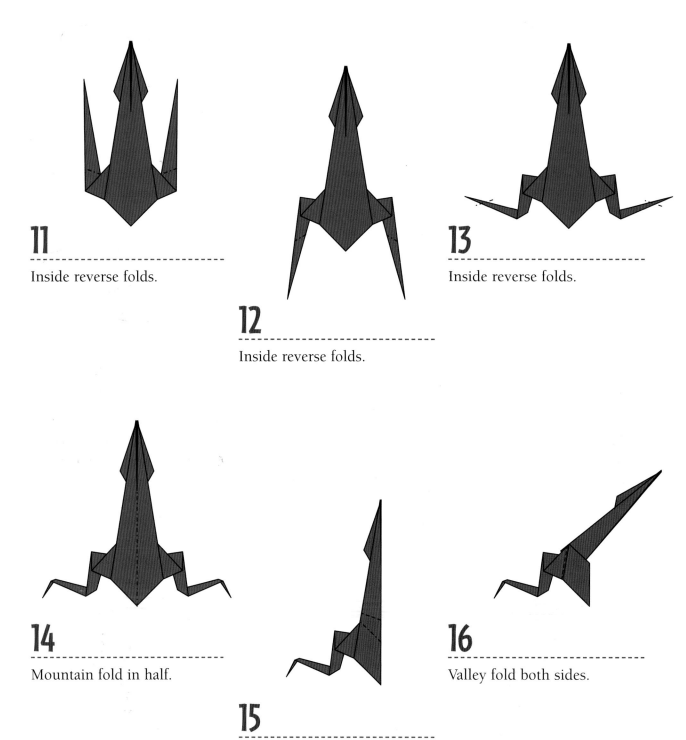

11

Inside reverse folds.

12

Inside reverse folds.

13

Inside reverse folds.

14

Mountain fold in half.

15

Crimp fold.

16

Valley fold both sides.

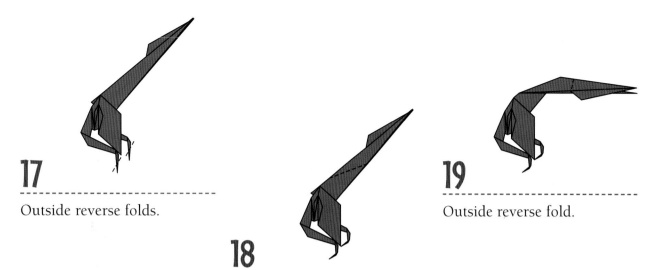

17

Outside reverse folds.

18

Outside reverse fold.

19

Outside reverse fold.

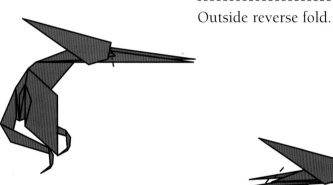

20

Mountain fold both sides down middle.

21

Mountain fold both sides and wrap to inside.

22

Completed part 1 of alien.

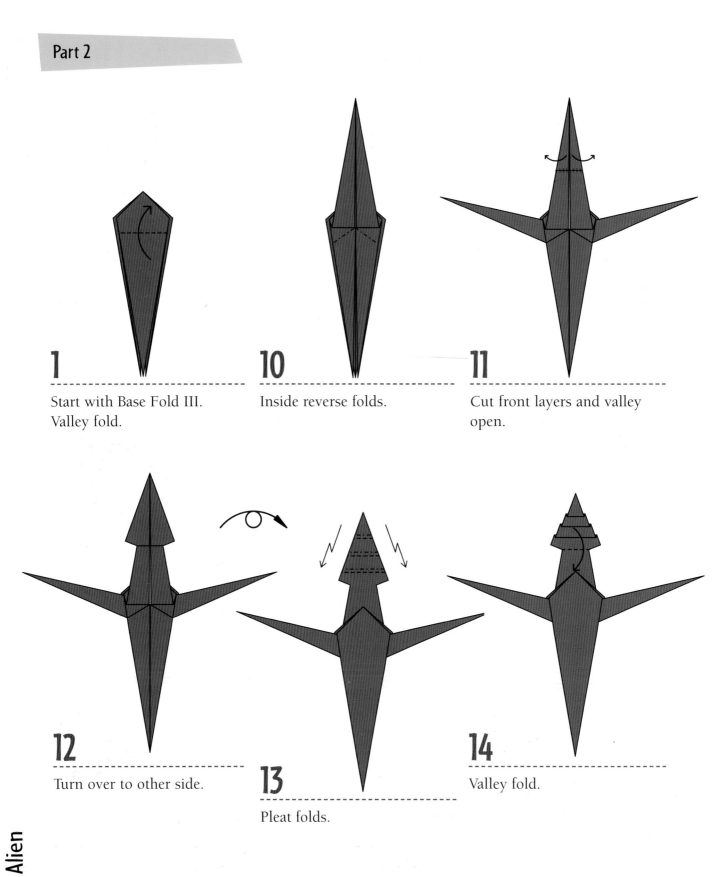

Part 2

1

Start with Base Fold III.
Valley fold.

10

Inside reverse folds.

11

Cut front layers and valley open.

12

Turn over to other side.

13

Pleat folds.

14

Valley fold.

15

Inside reverse folds.

16

Inside reverse folds.

17

Mountain fold in half.

18

Inside reverse folds.

19

Valley fold both sides.

20

Crimp fold.

21

Crimp fold.

22

Crimp fold.

23

Valley fold.

Alien

24

Turn over to other side.

25

Valley fold.

26

Completed part 2 of alien.

To Attach

1

Join both parts together as shown and apply glue to hold.

2

Completed Alien.

Monster Meet-up

Vampire Bat

Demon

Alien

Werewolf

Count Dracula

Frankenstein's Monster

King Ghidora

Wolfman

Creature from the Black Lagoon

Reptilia

Index

WITHDRAWN